Samuel French Acting Ed

MW00527048

You Make My Frame Shake!

12 Love Comedies Set at the Metropolitan Museum of Art

by Luigi Jannuzzi

SAMUELFRENCH.COM   SAMUELFRENCH.CO.UK

FOR PRODUCTION ENQUIRIES

UNITED STATES AND CANADA
Info@SamuelFrench.com
1-866-598-8449

UNITED KINGDOM AND EUROPE
Plays@SamuelFrench.co.uk
020-7255-4302

Each title is subject to availability from Samuel French, depending upon country of performance. Please be aware that *YOU MAKE MY FRAME SHAKE!* may not be licensed by Samuel French in your territory. Professional and amateur producers should contact the nearest Samuel French office or licensing partner to verify availability.

MUSIC USE NOTE

IMPORTANT BILLING AND CREDIT REQUIREMENTS

YOU MAKE MY FRAME SHAKE was developed/read/presented at:

The Metropolitan Theatre Company on February 10 & April 3, 2013 (Sessions at Weist-Barron, NYC). The director was Luigi Jannuzzi.

ACTORS . . . . .Charles F. Wagner IV, Dawn E. McGee,
Bruce Edward Barton, Louis Jannuzzi III,
Joseph Franchini, Katherine Puma, Jane Courtney,
Claire Buchignani, Mark Jannuzzi

The Theater Project (Union, NJ) on February 14, 2015. The director was Justin Bennett.

ACTORS . . . . Deborah Maclean, Kelley McAndrews,
Sean Day, James Morgan, Stewart Schneck,
Anna Marie Sell, Christopher J. Young

The Villagers Theatre (Somerset, NJ) on April 13, 2015. The producer was Lluana Jones and the director was Stephen Hirsekorn.

ACTORS . . . . Mary Lawrence, Stephen Hirsekorn,
Lydia Durham, Christopher W. Hall, Judy Wilson,
Harvey Rothman, Robert Cleary

The Theater Project (Union, NJ) on April 30, 2016. The director was Mark Spina.

ACTORS . . . . .Gary Glor, Anna Marie Sell,
Harry Patrick Christian, Angela Della Ventura,
Andre DeSandies, Lori Vega, Will Budnikov

Hudson Theatre Works (Weehawken, NJ) on May 14, 2018. The director was Luigi Jannuzzi.

ACTORS . . . . Catherine Ann Gale, Cassandra Giovane,
Kevin Cristaldi, Sara Parcespe,
T.C. Tanis, James Georgiades

ANDTheatre Company (NYC) on April 29 & May 20, 2018.

ACTORS . . . . .Janice L. Goldberg, Kristine Niven,
Jeremy Kareken, Mike Lawler,
Chima Chikazunga, Margaret Geraghty,
Matt Mezzacappa, Jeffery Sweet

CHARACTERS

Can be performed by 3 females and 3 males or by as many as 40 actors.
(Flexible and gender-blind casting.)

ACT ONE

Scene	F	M
Part I: Another Misguided Tour*	1	
Lusting After Monet	2	2
The Tray Picker-Upper in the Met Café*	1 (Either)	
Part II: Another Misguided Tour	1	
Dating Roman Art	2	3
Two Children Teasing a Cat*	1 (Either)	
Stuck in the Middle With You	2	2
Part III: Another Misguided Tour	1	
Another Fertility God Fugue	3	3

ACT TWO

Broken Eggs	1	1
Part IV: Another Misguided Tour	1	
Here Sphinxie, Sphinxie!	2	2
Part V: Another Misguided Tour	1	
The Art of Detention	3	2
Thought – A Love Story*		1
Part VI: Another Misguided Tour	1	
Joe and Helen Meet the Roman Art	3	3
Optional: Babes in the Bernini	1	1

*Monologue

Notes:
In case you need to cut a larger scene, the shorter option is *Babes in the Bernini*.
Another Misguided Tour I – VI is the framing device of one love-seeking tour guide. These scenes can also include many members of the cast as the tour. Be Creative!

AUTHOR'S NOTES

Casting is extremely flexible. And since this play is eight one-acts and four monologue comedies, there are many ways it may be presented. It can be performed with as few as six or as many as forty. Feel free to change genders for guards, curators, fertility gods, etc. A Catholic all-girls school in Princeton, New Jersey did the play with twenty females; and it was a hit! Why can't Aristotle or Poseidon be played by a woman?

Single Set: This is all that is needed. Set pieces should be kept to a minimum. The first production used only stools, black squares, and minimal props. Rely on the audience and their imagination to bring the rest. They will reward you for that opportunity.

Costumes can be as simple as everyone wearing black and using suggested props to elaborate the costumes. Though I think Aristotle (male or female) has to have a toga! Who doesn't like togas?

All pieces of artwork (over sixty items) are listed in the back of the book and on my website (www.LuigiJannuzzi.com) with links to the Met Museum for educational reasons. There's even a powerpoint. Feel free to use all the artwork. All photos were taken by me.

Projections and Transitions: Projections can be used if you have the technology. One production did not and the audience said that they did not miss anything. Or use multiple screens. One production used a single projection before each scene. Be creative!

Order of Scenes: I feel that this is the order in which the show runs best. It ends with the statues and will be your perfect ending.

CUT DOWN THE SHOW IF YOU NEED TO. I'd love to hear your ideas on what had to be cut to fit your venue. One idea is to cut a larger scene and put in the shorter optional scene "Babes in the Bernini."

Directing this play you will find that since it is divided into separate vignettes, the entire cast doesn't have to be there all the time, which is a lot easier on the cast and director.

Tone of the play: Warm, lively, fast, and fun! Please stay away from anger. There is none of that emotion written in this play. Anger is just not funny. Frustration is, but not anger. Yet amateur actors always go right for anger, which is the easiest emotion to act, and it ruins comedies all the time. Please show this paragraph to any who try. After playing anger, amateurs love to add curse words. Please do not allow that either. There are none in this play for a reason. It doesn't need any. It's a comedy.

Please go to my website and email any comments, questions, or pictures. I'd love to post them on my site and brag about your production and creativity. So if you are using a scene for forensics, a one-act competition, or in a collection of one-acts, I'd love to hear how it went. (Especially if you put the tour director parts together as a single monologue for forensics.)

Raising the awareness of Art through the use of Comedy and trying to create in a verbal medium (Theatre) a hunger for a visual medium (Paintings) is one of the objects of the show.

Have fun. It was fun writing these plays and directing them. Audiences howl and applaud often. From Princeton professors to middle school performers, it makes them laugh.

Break a Frame!

– Luigi Jannuzzi

Special Thanks to: Amy Rose Marsh, Garrett Anderson, David Kimple, Nicole Matte, David Geer, Casey McLain, Alejandra Venancio, Coryn Carson, Jonah Rosen, Ryan Pointer, Tyler Mullen, Bruce Lazarus, Chris Kam, Sarah Weber, Elizabeth Minski, Ali Tesluk, Abbie Van Nostrand, Nathan Collins, and all at Samuel French Inc.; the late William (Bill) Talbot; the late Alleen Hussung; The Dramatist Guild, especially Deborah Murad, Esq., Ralph Sevush, Esq., David H. Faux, Esq.; The Author's Guild; Nancy E. Wolff, Esq. at Cowan, DeBaets, Abrahams & Sheppard LLP; Mario Fratti for all his advice and confidence; Louis and Mark Jannuzzi for all their support; the Princeton University Library and Deborah Maclean for a wonderful dinner party reading of an early version with Gloria Falzer, Valerie Stack Dodge, Avery Hart, Judy Dowd, Dave Groveman, Paul Mantell, Dennis DaPrile, and Stew Schneck.

Douglas L. Caskey and a Goshen College Peace Play award for the one-act *Here Sphinxie, Sphinxie!*; Forge directors Frank Licato and Greg Erbach; Theatre Project director Mark Spina; Villagers producer Lluana Jones; Walter Placzek; Brannon Whitehead; Michael and Candace Gallagher; Elizabeth Rothan; Tim McFadden; Janice Baldwin and Christina Kosyla and their drama students at the Stuart County Day School of the Sacred Heart in Princeton, New Jersey for such wonderful feedback about an early version; Luis Angulo of La_Designs for spectacular creative designs; and the Metropolitan Museum of Art.

"The mind can not absorb what the rear end can not endure."

– Unknown

Another Misguided Tour

PART I

CHARACTERS

WOMAN – female, perfectly dressed

SETTING

Bare stage with two blank white canvases upon two tripods:
one left and one right stage

TIME

Present

*For a list of artwork in this scene, please see the back of the book.

(Lights rise on a very bubbly **WOMAN** *giving a tour to imaginary people that may or may not be there.)*

WOMAN. Good afternoon, everyone.

(To audience member.) Oh, love your blouse. Very bold. *(To another audience member.)* And your cameo. Charming.

(To all.) Hey, if we can take this chicness, bunch together, and follow my Gucci heels, your tour of *(Changes to small voice.)* the little tiny, itsy-bitsy, *(Uses a deep voice.)* broad and breathtaking *(Normal voice.)* world of Nature and Landscape, like Frederic Edwin Church's 1859 masterpiece, "The Heart of the Andes," will be positively...WOW!

(Pause. Big smile.)

Follow me!

(Referring to Albert Bierstadt's "The Rocky Mountains, Lander's Peak.")

How do you feel looking at this? Tense? Anxious?

(Pause.)

Well, you will if you look deeply into the detail of Albert Bierstadt's "The Rocky Mountains, Lander's Peak." You can almost hear the birds. Hear the birds?

(Does bird sound.)

But look bottom middle, a gopher is peering out of a hole unaware of the adolescent with bow and arrow and something to prove. Bottom left, another gopher stands helplessly watching the teenage hunter size up his rodent buddy. "Don't shoot him, don't shoot my buddy!"

(To rodent.) Look at you, you little rodent. You are such a cutie. Yes you are.

(To audience.) Ever feel like that? No?

(To painting.) See, it doesn't have to be total helplessness. It can just be that feeling you get when you owe an agency twenty percent of your salary when all they did for you was to find the notice on the museum's website. Or a modeling agency fifty percent of anything you find yourself, and they're not even looking for you. Or the mail you keep ignoring because you've maxed out three credit cards to try to make yourself marketable to the new love of your life whom you're waiting for to call, as he promised, while you fill up the time giving tours of anxious landscape art. Oh, I love this painting.

(Pause.)

Follow me!

Lusting After Monet

CHARACTERS

(in order of appearance)

CLAUDE MONET – male
CAMILLE MONET – female
ERNEST HOSCHEDÉ – male
ALICE HOSCHEDÉ – female

SETTING

Bare stage with park bench, easel, and small table

For a list of artwork in this scene, please see the back of the book.

(Music begins* and lights rise on **CLAUDE MONET** *setting up a canvas to paint his wife,* **CAMILLE MONET***, who is standing near a bench. The set is a bare stage with a garden bench, an easel with canvas, and a small table with painting supplies.)*

(Actors can be dressed in black with different hats: **CLAUDE** *a beret,* **CAMILLE** *a black hat,* **ALICE HOSCHEDÉ** *a white sun hat, and* **ERNEST HOSCHEDÉ** *a formal top hat. See the painting "Camille Monet on a Garden Bench" for the hats that the four are wearing.)*

(Also try to pronounce names in French; they sound more romantic, especially **ERNEST** *and* **ALICE***.)*

CLAUDE. Camille Monet, YOU.

> *(Pause.)*

You shall sit there, I shall stand here...and we shall capture your beauty with my brush. How's that sound?

CAMILLE. *(Sits on bench.)* Kiss, kiss.

CLAUDE. Wink, wink.

> *(***CAMILLE** *giggles.)*

Oh, and look who's coming.

ERNEST. Sorry, I'm late.

CLAUDE. You...shall stand behind my beautiful wife and smile. Thus adding contrast.

ERNEST. I would be delighted.

---

*A license to produce *You Make My Frame Shake!* does not include a performance license for any third-party or copyrighted music. Licensees should create an original composition or use music in the public domain. For further information, please see Music Use Note on page 3.

CAMILLE. Hello Ernest.

CLAUDE. Oh. And look who else is here.

ALICE. Sorry, so sorry. He drove, what else need I say.

CLAUDE. No problem. We are ready to begin?

> (**ALICE** *moves near the canvas. She is* **CLAUDE**'s *assistant. She begins opening tubes, putting colors on palette, and arranging brushes. Or she mimes this.*)

CAMILLE. Claude, this is just brief?

CLAUDE. A brief sketch.

CAMILLE. Really?

CLAUDE. I'm just interested in the form. And NOW...we begin!

> (*Pause.*)

ALICE. *(Whispers.)* Claude, do you know that the more I think about you...

CLAUDE. Alice, stop it.

ALICE. The more I think you're all I think about.

CLAUDE. *(To* **ALICE**.*)* They may hear you.

ALICE. I don't care.

CLAUDE. I do.

ALICE. Have you talked to Camille?

CLAUDE. I haven't.

ERNEST. I can't believe I'm in this painting with you.

CAMILLE. SHH...

ERNEST. Think about it.

CAMILLE. I'm not.

ERNEST. It's fate!

CAMILLE. Yes, yes but.

ERNEST. Have you spoken to him?

CAMILLE. It's not the time to speak to him.

ERNEST. Of course not. After he captures your beauty, then.

CAMILLE. You're making me blush.

ERNEST. Blush!

CAMILLE. I don't want to blush.

ERNEST. I want to see you blush.

CAMILLE. No. There will be no blushing in this painting. I want to be radiant.

ERNEST. Blushing could be radiant.

CAMILLE. Please, Ernest. Please, be patient.

ALICE. It should really be you and I in this painting, you know.

CLAUDE. It will come.

ALICE. When?

CLAUDE. Someday.

ALICE. Soon?

CLAUDE. Very soon.

ALICE. Look at her thinking she is the object of your eye, when I am.

CLAUDE. Absolutely.

ALICE. Then why are you looking at her?

CLAUDE. I'm trying to paint her.

ALICE. Look at me.

CLAUDE. How am I supposed to look at you and paint her?

ALICE. Why not?

CLAUDE. Because that doesn't make sense.

ALICE. Put my face on hers.

CLAUDE. That's insane.

ALICE. And your face on his.

CLAUDE. No.

ALICE. Give her my smile.

CLAUDE. No.

ALICE. My eyes.

CLAUDE. No.

ALICE. An ear.

CLAUDE. Stop it!

ALICE. Then very crooked teeth.

CLAUDE. I can't concentrate.

ALICE. I don't want you to.

CLAUDE. Well, you're doing a good job. Red. I need more red.

CAMILLE. *(To* **CLAUDE.***)* Why do you need more red?

ALICE. More red coming up.

CLAUDE. I just think more red.

CAMILLE. Am I blushing?

CLAUDE. Not particularly.

CAMILLE. Unparticularly? Am I blushing unparticularly? 'Cause I don't want to blush unparticularly either.

CLAUDE. You're perfect.

ALICE. Here's your red. Why did you say that?

CLAUDE. Say what?

ALICE. "She's perfect." She's not perfect, I am perfect, say it.

CLAUDE. You are perfect.

CAMILLE. *(To* **CLAUDE.***)* Is that good?

CLAUDE. Perfect. I mean…impeccable.

ERNEST. It's been three days since we've been alone.

CAMILLE. Sixty-one hours.

ERNEST. Twenty-four minutes.

CAMILLE & ERNEST. Six seconds.

> **(CAMILLE** *and* **ERNEST** *gasp, turn, look at each other, then turn back to pose.)*

CLAUDE. Sponge.

ALICE. *(Handing* **CLAUDE** *sponge.)* Sponge.

> **(CLAUDE** *sponges painting.)*

It's been two and a half days since I've seen you.

CLAUDE. I can't think about that, while I'm thinking about this.

ALICE. I want you to think about that, not think about this.

CLAUDE. I can't think about anything other than this, while I'm doing this.

ALICE. If you really loved me, you would think about that, not think about this while you're doing this.

CLAUDE. Is it possible to not think about something while you are trying to do it?

ALICE. Then think about this.

> (**ALICE** *goes behind the canvas, pressing against and trying to kiss* **CLAUDE**.)

Kiss me.

> (*At the same time, seeing both* **CLAUDE** *and* **ALICE** *behind canvas,* **ERNEST** *tries to kiss* **CAMILLE**.)

ERNEST. Kiss me now!

CLAUDE. (*Pushing* **ALICE** *away.*) No!

CAMILLE. (*Pushing* **ERNEST** *away.*) My lipstick!

> (**CLAUDE**'*s brush hits canvas.* **CAMILLE**'*s lipstick has smeared.*)

CLAUDE. Look what you made me do?

CAMILLE. My lips. They've smeared all over my face?

CLAUDE. There's a big blotch of red where her face is.

ALICE. Oh no.

ERNEST. Oh no.

ALICE. Look what I've done.

ERNEST. Look what I've done.

CAMILLE. Watch this, I will cover it by raising my hand.

CLAUDE. Hmm, watch this; I will cover it by painting her raising her hand.

CAMILLE. He's preoccupied.

CLAUDE. That big swatch could be her sleeve.

CAMILLE. Ernest?

CLAUDE. Genius.

ERNEST. Yes?

CLAUDE. Genius move.

CAMILLE. Give me your handkerchief.

CLAUDE. Brilliant!

CAMILLE. The handkerchief now.

CLAUDE. Now blend.

CAMILLE. From your topcoat pocket.

CLAUDE. I will blend in that red under her eyes.

ERNEST. Here!

CLAUDE. Around her mouth.

CAMILLE. I will hold this in my right hand.

CLAUDE. The other eye.

CAMILLE. Wipe a bit.

CLAUDE. I'm blending.

CAMILLE. Wiping.

CLAUDE. Look at me blend. Ha ha...

CAMILLE. Keeping my arm arched I can wipe on cue.

CLAUDE. And in order for it to counteract, I will put red in her bonnet, bouquet, bench, background, so much they won't even notice the red on her face.

ALICE. Geraniums. Put geraniums in the background.

CLAUDE. Yes. Yes, geraniums...hundreds, they'll absorb the red.

CAMILLE. *(To* **ERNEST.***)* What? What is this inside your handkerchief, Ernest?

ERNEST. It is a note, read it.

CLAUDE. Too many geraniums?

ALICE. Too much.

CLAUDE. You think?

ALICE. Look what you've done. Put someone in, standing there.

CLAUDE. What do you mean?

ALICE. ME! Put Me in.

CLAUDE. No.

ALICE. Yes.

CLAUDE. NO.

ALICE. Me, looking at the geraniums. It will deflect color.

CLAUDE. That would even it.

ALICE. With a parasol.

CLAUDE. Hmmm.

ALICE. A beautiful dress, elegant, flowing.

CLAUDE. White, alive.

ALICE. Reaching out to the flowers. 'Cause you are those flowers. That will be our painting.

CLAUDE. It works.

ALICE. Let her have the foreground. But make her lifeless, gray, dull.

CLAUDE. Sad, it would downplay the red.

ALICE. Very sad.

CLAUDE. If her lips were closer, her eyes.

ALICE. Glazed.

CLAUDE. Her eyebrows.

ALICE. Drooping, make them droop. And in the background put all of the sunlight on MEEEE!

CLAUDE. Yes.

ALICE. Keep him in the dark too.

CLAUDE. Absolutely.

ALICE. Shadows crawling around them.

CLAUDE. With her hand away from her mouth, she can hold whatever it is she's holding. What is it that she's reading?

CAMILLE. I've read it.

ERNEST. Read it aloud.

CAMILLE. *(Reading.)* "I want to be with you forever. Love Ernest."

ERNEST. That is how I feel.

ALICE. Pay no attention to her. My parasol, make it as if the sun is shining just on it.

CAMILLE. I shall hold this note in my hand forever.

ERNEST. Yes.

CAMILLE. And though I seem to lean away from you, it's 'cause I cannot read the note. The sun seems to have gone behind the tree.

CLAUDE. A thicker brush.

ALICE. *(Hands* **CLAUDE** *another brush.)* Thicker brush.

> **(CLAUDE** *brushes wildly, as if dusting the canvas.)*

CLAUDE. There!

ALICE. Love it.

CLAUDE. A triangle of three.

ALICE. Yes.

ERNEST. How's it going, Claude?

CAMILLE. Are we close, Claude?

CLAUDE. We are finished with the first impression.

CAMILLE. Good.

ERNEST. Excellent.

ALICE. Wonderful.

CLAUDE. And as you know, I do not allow anyone to see it.

> **(CLAUDE** *puts white sheet over canvas.)*

CAMILLE. I understand.

ERNEST. We understand.

> **(ALICE** *crosses from downstage left to upstage right of the bench.)*

ALICE. So in the painting, I'm going to be standing right about here?

CAMILLE. You?

ERNEST. You?

ALICE. Yes me.

CAMILLE. Claude, why is Alice going to be standing there?

CLAUDE. She is in it for a purpose.

CAMILLE. And the purpose is?

CLAUDE. Balance. She balances out the purpose. I think... that's right.

CAMILLE. That doesn't make sense.

ERNEST. Wait a second.

ALICE. And I balance the geraniums.

CAMILLE & ERNEST. GERANIUMS!

ALICE. That compliment the sunlight.

CAMILLE. Shouldn't I be doing that?

ERNEST. If anyone should be brilliant, shouldn't it be Camille?

ALICE. To contrast your shadowy images.

CAMILLE. Am I in shadow, Claude?

CLAUDE. No.

ERNEST. Oh no Claude, I get the impression we're lurking in shadows.

CLAUDE. No.

ERNEST. Are we lurking, Claude?

CLAUDE. No, no...there is no lurking.

CAMILLE. Sounds like lurking.

ALICE. With my dazzling parasol.

CAMILLE. I want a parasol.

ALICE. But you have a note, or whatever that is that you're reading.

(**CAMILLE** *and* **ERNEST** *gasp.*)

And what, in your hand, are you reading?

CAMILLE. I don't know, I can't read it. I'm in the shadows.

ERNEST. Yes, we're lurking here with an unreadable note.

ALICE. While I in my white bonnet.

CAMILLE & ERNEST. White bonnet?

ALICE. Elegant flowery dress.

CAMILLE & ERNEST. Elegant?

CAMILLE. Claude, I'm sorry, I must have a word with you.

ERNEST. Claude, I must speak with you too.

CLAUDE. Speak all you want. You only have one right. To look at it when it is finished!

ERNEST. But what it sounds like, Claude, my god.

CLAUDE. From whom?

CAMILLE. Your assistant, your wife, your friend.

CLAUDE. None of whom has seen it. You are judging something that doesn't exit.

CAMILLE. Oh.

ERNEST. Oh.

ALICE. OH.

CLAUDE. You do not trust me?

CAMILLE. No that's not.

ERNEST. NO we.

ALICE. No it's not that.

CLAUDE. Do you not feel my talents can portray you honestly?

CAMILLE. Sorry.

ERNEST. Sorry.

ALICE. Sorry.

CLAUDE. Yes, the portrait will be divided shadow and light, contain geraniums, and Camille will be center. And yes it will be magnificent, colorful, balanced. And in the end even artists will look upon it and say, "Look at Claude Monet's gorgeous portrait of Camille Monet on a garden bench, that handsome smiling gentleman, and the elegant lady, with the perfect parasol. Need I say more?

CAMILLE. I didn't know I was center.

ERNEST. Thank you for the handsome smile.

ALICE. And the perfect parasol.

CLAUDE. I need two months. I still have to finish our son on his hobby horse.

CAMILLE. Claude, I have a headache, I must head inside.

CLAUDE. Well, I have to put all this away.

ERNEST. I'll take Camille inside.

CAMILLE. Yes, Ernest, later.

ALICE. I'll stay and clean up.

CLAUDE. Thank you Alice.

ERNEST. Alice, I will see you later.

ALICE. Yes Ernest, I will see you later.

> (**CAMILLE** *and* **ERNEST** *exit. Pause.* **ALICE** *sits on bench.* **CLAUDE** *is putting paints away.*)

That went well.

CLAUDE. It did.

ALICE. You have your form.

CLAUDE. I do.

ALICE. I have my place.

CLAUDE. In the painting. Surprising.

ALICE. Claude?

CLAUDE. Yes.

ALICE. I want to be center.

CLAUDE. Not now.

ALICE. When?

CLAUDE. Soon.

ALICE. How soon?

CLAUDE. Someday.

ALICE. But when I am in the center, Claude, will I be in the shadows like poor Camille? 'Cause I don't want that Claude. I don't want to be the lady in the shadows on the bench. I want to be in the sunlight with a parasol but centered, Claude, centered!

CLAUDE. It will come.

ALICE. When?

CLAUDE. Someday.

ALICE. Soon?

CLAUDE. Very soon.

> (**ALICE** *picks up something from under the bench.*)

ALICE. Claude?

CLAUDE. Yes?

ALICE. It's coming faster then we thought, Claude.

CLAUDE. Why? Why do you say that?

ALICE. Because Claude, you should read this note I just found, in the shadows, under the bench, that the sad centered woman dropped.

> (**CLAUDE** *crosses, reads note.* **CLAUDE** *looks at* **ALICE***. Both gasp at each other. Smile. Pause. Then kiss.*)
>
> (*Lights fade.*)
>
> (*Blackout.*)
>
> [*Fact: In 1878, Claude and Camille Monet moved in with Ernest and Alice Hoschedé. After Camille died in 1879, Ernest left Alice, and Claude and Alice married.*]

The Tray Picker-Upper
in the Met Café

CHARACTERS

CAFETERIA WORKER – male or female

SETTING

Bare stage

TIME

Contemporary

*For a list of artwork in this scene, please see the back of the book.

(Lights rise on **CAFETERIA WORKER** *standing center stage but with head turned looking offstage left.)*

*(***CAFETERIA WORKER*** *looks at audience.)*

CAFETERIA WORKER. *(To off-left.)* The Trays? Place them on top of any garbage bin. Thanks.

(To audience.) I can't talk too long, I'm working. But it's true. It did happen. And it happened 'cause I love art. 'Cause, as Andy Warhol believed, if you hang around art and artists long enough, you too will be famous.

(To off-right.) Excuse me?

(Pause.)

Well, if you feel that yogurt seal was broken, tell any cashier, they'll give you another one.

You're welcome.

(To audience.) I'm thirty, been an art lover for ten years since I've been blessed to work here. I'm trays, garbage and floor duty. And I'm also convinced that it's 'cause I do my job well that it happened. This is exactly where I was standing. He, I cringe when I have to pronounce his name 'cause I always get it wrong. So let's just call him "the artist." "The artist" was sitting there. And he walked over and he gave it to me. And that's it. He walked out; never saw him before or again. And I like it. I think the drawing looks just like me. Then one of the curators comes to me and asks if I saw the artist. I say, "Yeah, he just left." The curator's disappointed. I ask, "How famous and who is the artist?" And that's when, just like I told the news reporters, the curator said, "I'm sure you wouldn't know or be interested in any of his art." And then I showed the curator the drawing the artist did of me, collecting the trays the artistic way I do. And the curator asked, "May I see

that?" I hand it to him. He looks at it for about ten minutes. Really, about ten minutes. His mouth opening more and more as he looks at it. Then he starts walking away with it. I say, "Hey, excuse me, that's mine." He says, "No, I'm sorry, this belongs to the museum." I say, "It's a drawing of me!" And that's when he said exactly what I told the reporters: "A person in your station of life, cannot begin to understand this the way I do. Do you understand?" That's when I grabbed it from him. And it ripped. In half.

(Pause.)

And that's when, in our crowded café, he started screaming, "You're fired! You're fired!" I grabbed the other half and I ran. That was yesterday. Today it's all over the news. It seems a reporter was following the artist. So the curator is suspended with pay, the artist has now offered to do a portrait of me. I said, "I'd be delighted." My favorite painting here is called "A Waitress in Duval's Restaurant" by Renoir. So I think my portrait should be called "Tray Picker-Upper in the Met Café." What do you think?

(Pause.)

I now have a lawyer/agent since ten this morning who is negotiating my case and the lease of the "future" portrait to the Met. So life is good. I'm back to work. And maybe Andy Warhol's right, if you hang around art and artists long enough, you too will be famous. Plus I got two halves of a drawing and a portrait. Not bad for an art lover in my station.

(To imaginary person off-left.) The fruit? Sure, go through the cash register and to the right.

(Pause.)

You're welcome.

(To audience.) I better get back to work picking up some trays. You never know who's here today.

(Lights fade. Blackout.)

Another Misguided Tour

PART II

(Referring to "Siyotanka courting flute" in Musical Instruments.)

WOMAN. This is a Native American courting flute. It is made of Catlinite, named for George Catlin, the American landscape artist, who not only has the most paintings in the White House, but who gave up his law practice in order to document the cause of Native Americans. He has 500 paintings, organized the first Wild West shows, and lost all his money doing both. But when you look at this flute you have to think that he tried. Like I did with my flute in my state's beauty pageant –

(Pause.)

– only to come up with that second-place ribbon that I stare at every night, dangling from my desk lamp wondering, "Will that be the highlight of my career? Was that my fifteen seconds of fame?" Well, I thank you George Catlin, and we salute you and your flute. Wow! It's quite inspirational, isn't it?

(Pause.)

Follow me.

Dating Roman Art

CHARACTERS

(in order of appearance)

ATLAS – male

POSEIDON – male or female

HERCULES – male

SOFIA – female

SETTING

Bare stage, three pedestals

TIME

Contemporary

*For a list of artwork in this scene, please see the back of the book.

(Lights rise on museum and three statues of **ATLAS**, **POSEIDON**, *and* **HERCULES**. **ATLAS** *is holding up the world. A young woman [***SOFIA***] who is also a statue enters, smiles, sneaks up to statue of* **ATLAS** *and grabs* **ATLAS** *under his loincloth.)*

SOFIA. Got you.

ATLAS. AHHHHH!

SOFIA. Put the world down.

ATLAS. I'm putting it down.

SOFIA. I'll squeeze.

ATLAS. It's down. It's down.

SOFIA. You want to lose these?

ATLAS. No.

POSEIDON. Whoa!

ATLAS. Oh, please let go.

HERCULES. Should I call security?

ATLAS. No.

POSEIDON. Somebody's in trouble.

HERCULES. And this is why I don't date anyone steady.

*(***SOFIA*** drags ***ATLAS*** off pedestal, then lets go.)*

SOFIA. I had...to hear it from...someone else?

ATLAS. Hear what?

SOFIA. You took someone on a tour last night?

POSEIDON. Ut-oh.

HERCULES. Oops.

POSEIDON. I warned you.

HERCULES. I did too.

SOFIA. Stay out of this.

POSEIDON & HERCULES. Just saying.

SOFIA. Both of you.

ATLAS. I was asked.

SOFIA. By whom?

ATLAS. The new assistant Roman curator of statues. I forgot his name.

SOFIA. I know, the new young cute guy with the hair all spiked.

ATLAS. Yeah, that guy.

SOFIA. I don't like him.

ATLAS. They were a statue short, they needed three statues.

SOFIA. Oh, and were these the other two?

> (**POSEIDON** *and* **HERCULES** *cover their crotches with their hands.*)

ATLAS. Yes they were.

SOFIA. I should have known.

ATLAS. So I said I would help.

SOFIA. *(To* **POSEIDON** *and* **HERCULES**.*)* You both don't have any friends who aren't dating someone?

POSEIDON. He volunteered.

HERCULES. That's right.

SOFIA. That's right. You volunteered. You didn't have to, you did.

ATLAS. He's the assistant curator, he's in charge of us, he needed a volunteer for one hour.

SOFIA. I heard it took three hours.

ATLAS. Not even two.

POSEIDON. An hour and a half.

HERCULES. When you factor in drinks,

POSEIDON. The hors d'oeuvres.

HERCULES. I thought the hors d'oeuvres were good.

POSEIDON. Surprisingly.

SOFIA. SHUT UP!

> (**POSEIDON** *and* **HERCULES** *both put other hand over mouth.*)

And I hear she's young.

POSEIDON. Hey, didn't the museum just open?

HERCULES. Atlas, Poseidon's right. Customers any second.

SOFIA. Very attractive.

POSEIDON. If Atlas is sent to storage, won't we all get sent?

HERCULES. Atlas, Poseidon's right, let's get posed.

SOFIA. And an Amazon woman, huh? Huh?

POSEIDON. I hear someone coming. Someone's coming.

SOFIA. I know about you and Amazons.

HERCULES. Get ready, Atlas!

SOFIA. I know the history of you and Amazon maidens.

POSEIDON. Atlas, get the world.

ATLAS. I'm sorry.

SOFIA. Bull, you're sorry; I hear you had a great time.

(**POSEIDON** *and* **HERCULES** *nod.*)

POSEIDON. Altas, apologize again.

HERCULES. Promise her anything.

POSEIDON. Say you'll marry her.

SOFIA. Atlas, are you listening?

ATLAS. I'm very, very, very sorry.

POSEIDON. We're doomed.

HERCULES. Do something. I can't go back to storage.

ATLAS. Sofia?

(**SOFIA** *bursts into tears.*)

Sofia?

POSEIDON. Oh no.

HERCULES. She's out of control.

ATLAS. Please Sofia?

SOFIA. I am an idiot, I'm such an idiot.

POSEIDON. Atlas?

HERCULES. He doesn't even hear us.

ATLAS. Sofia, you are a beautiful statue.

SOFIA. Stop it.

ATLAS. Look at you. You're a young beautiful Roman maiden full of life.

SOFIA. I'm a tart.

ATLAS. You are not a tart.

SOFIA. You'll never marry me.

ATLAS. Listen, you go back to storage room twenty-four.

SOFIA. Twenty-five –

ATLAS. Twenty-five, and you wait for me there.

SOFIA. That's what you always say.

ATLAS. You and I are going to have a talk tonight.

SOFIA. We never have a talk, we have sex.

ATLAS. Well, tonight we're going to have a talk.

> (**POSEIDON** *and* **HERCULES** *both signaling to each other, "Oh sure."*)

SOFIA. *(To* **POSEIDON** *and* **HERCULES**.*)* SHUT UP!

> (**POSEIDON** *and* **HERCULES** *both put one hand on crotch and the other hand over eyes and mouth.*)

ATLAS. Sofia?

> (**SOFIA** *turns around to* **ATLAS**.*)*

Sofia?

> *(She cries more.)*

Sofia, listen to me.

SOFIA. I just sit in that storage room by myself with those sarcophagi, three headless guys, that chariot going nowhere, and I wait...I wait for someone to talk to, for you to come by, for something to lift my crappy, dusty, little life out of that pit of the Julio-Claudian period, where I don't even belong, and then that statuette of a veiled masked dancer comes by, whoever the hell she is, and has the audacity to tell me you were having a great time on the roof garden with some Amazon maiden... Oh god! *(Cries.)*

ATLAS. I know it's not fair.

SOFIA. No.

ATLAS. It's not right.

SOFIA. No.

ATLAS. Well it's going to change right now.

SOFIA. It is?

ATLAS. Before we're all in room twenty-four.

POSEIDON. With the sarcophagi.

HERCULES. And the headless guys.

POSEIDON. Oh god!

ATLAS. Yes it is. And I'm going to change it.

SOFIA. How?

ATLAS. I'm going to tell that young curator –

SOFIA. Yeah.

ATLAS. To get you out of that room.

SOFIA. Really?

ATLAS. I'll demand.

SOFIA. You will?

ATLAS. That you.

POSEIDON. I almost believe him.

ATLAS. As my beloved.

HERCULES. Shhh.

ATLAS. As the real reason I hold up this world –

POSEIDON. You go guy.

HERCULES. Yeah!

ATLAS. Must be within my sight.

> (**POSEIDON** *and* **HERCULES** *clap,* **SOFIA** *glances over, they stop, resume poses. Pause.* **SOFIA** *stands.)*

SOFIA. Well, okay.

ATLAS. And I'm doing it today, so he remembers I did him a favor, and he can repay me.

SOFIA. Promise?

ATLAS. Cross my heart

POSEIDON & HERCULES. *(To each other.)* Of stone.

> (**SOFIA** *looks at* **POSEIDON** *and* **HERCULES,** *they smile sheepishly.*)

POSEIDON. I hear customers.

HERCULES. I do too.

SOFIA. I better go.

ATLAS. See you tonight.

SOFIA. You better be there.

ATLAS. I'm there.

SOFIA. And I'm sorry.

ATLAS. I'm sorry, too. Let me just get the world here.

> *(Picks up world.)*

There we go.

> *(Back on pedestal.)*

Back and ready to go.

SOFIA. *(To* **POSEIDON** *and* **HERCULES.***)* I'm sorry, too.

POSEIDON. No problem.

HERCULES. Apology accepted.

POSEIDON. Very understandable.

HERCULES. Absolutely.

SOFIA. The three of you are so lucky to be up here, highlighted, around this beautiful bubbling fountain in the sun and sky with live people around.

POSEIDON. Hopefully someday.

HERCULES. You'll be bubbling with us.

ATLAS. Sofia, I am carrying the weight of it for you today.

SOFIA. I know you are, Atlas, I know you are.

POSEIDON, HERCULES & ATLAS. Here they come.

SOFIA. Customer!

> (**SOFIA** *runs off as* **FEMALE CUSTOMER** *enters, crosses up to* **ATLAS.***)*

CUSTOMER. Oh Atlas.

(**CUSTOMER** *points to and near* **ATLAS**.)

Aren't you cute. And those muscles!

(**SOFIA** *jealously looks back into room with scowl.*)

SOFIA. *(Yells from off.)* Keep your hands off the Sculpture!

(**CUSTOMER** *looks around, begins to walk off.*)

(Lights fade. Blackout.)

[Note: A painted exercise ball makes a terrific bouncy globe.]

Two Children
Teasing a Cat

CHARACTERS

LISA – female

or

LEO – male

SETTING

Bare stage

TIME

Present

*For a list of artwork in this scene, please see the back of the book.

*(**LISA** enters, very frustrated. Please don't play this angry. Frustrated is funny, angry is not.)*

LISA. Right now, I am going to talk to the curator of this museum. And I'm going to get the curator of this museum to change the title of my painting. Because I'm sorry. I'm very very sorry, but, I love my cat.

(Frustrated, not angry.) So why? Why did I let anyone paint me teasing the cat that I love?!

(Just a little lower.) First: What kind of man paints cats? That's weird. But Mother says, "Annibale Carracci is one of the most famous Italian painters. He's usually painting Jesus and the Saints and he wants to grace the Ranuzzi family with a picture of you, your brother and our cat. And it's going to be a morality picture where we are supposed to be teasing our cat and the cat is about to scratch us to show everyone not to tease cats." Here's where it backfires. Four Hundred Years Ago: everyone understood we were a message picture. Today: everyone thinks we are just harassing a cat. The title of our painting is not: "Don't do this." The title is: "Two Children Teasing a Cat." We are now poster children for animal cruelty. We are the meanest bastards at the Met. Mothers and fathers can't explain us. Every day we hear: "That's terrible." "Those mean kids." "That poor kitty."

(Pause.)

They're saying I'm a psychopath! I'm trapped in 400-year-old psycho-art! Yeah, laugh all you want. You're not the one in counseling four times a month. I belong to a group called: Psycho-Art. It's for people trapped in art interpreted by today's clientele as psychotic. We have a large group too. It's me, all the guys from "The Abduction of the Sabine Women," the Messerschmidt sculpture: "A Hypocrite and a Slanderer," there are a lot of rabbit hunters, unicorn stalkers, some demons. A big group. And it's getting bigger. The painting of Salome with the head of Saint John the Baptist stopped by the other night. But it is partly her fault. I mean, she does carry the head around.

(Pause.)

Anyway, we meet every Monday, near the cannibal art in Oceania. Give your card to any usher if you're interested. I have to go. I'm late to the curator meeting. Though, he's not going to change anything. We have a saying here at the Met, "Nothing changes once we're dry."

Wish me luck!

(She exits. Blackout.)

Stuck in the Middle With You

(or How Monsignor Lavoisier Keeps His Head)

CHARACTERS
(in order of appearance)

ANTOINE-LAURENT LAVOISIER – male
MARIE LAVOISIER – female, Antoine's wife
CUSTOMER 1
CURATOR
CUSTOMER 2*
CUSTOMER 3*

*can be **CUSTOMER 1** and **CURATOR** in disguise

SETTING
Bare stage with desk, two chairs

TIME
Contemporary

*For a list of artwork in this scene, please see the back of the book.

(We hear some French music playing* as lights rise on a giant frame, inside of which **ANTOINE** *is writing at his desk downstage left.* **MARIE** *is in a chair upstage right and is talking in her sleep. She is having a nightmare.)*

(Actors can be dressed in black with different hats. **ANTOINE** *is in a white wig and* **MARIE** *is in a wig like the one in the painting "Antoine-Laurent Lavoisier and his Wife.")*

MARIE. *(Talking while sleeping.)* Antoine!

ANTOINE. One second.

MARIE. France is falling.

ANTOINE. Right with you.

MARIE. The guillotine.

ANTOINE. Mmm mmmmm.

MARIE. Even if you are...the father of chemistry!

ANTOINE. *(Turns to* **MARIE.***)* Marie? You're talking in your sleep.

MARIE. THEY HATE US!

ANTOINE. You're yelling in your sleep.

MARIE. You're a tax collector.

ANTOINE. Wake up, Marie. No one is looking for us except maybe art lovers.

MARIE. *(Waking up.)* Oh, Antoine. I go to sleep afraid, I wake afraid.

ANTOINE. Marie, get ready. The museum just opened.

---

*A license to produce *You Make My Frame Shake!* does not include a performance license for any third-party or copyrighted music. Licensees should create an original composition or use music in the public domain. For further information, please see Music Use Note on page 3.

MARIE. But suppose they cut off your head?

ANTOINE. They can't cut off my head again.

MARIE. They can cut your head out of the painting.

ANTOINE. Marie, we are one of the most famous paintings in America!

MARIE. We have to run Antoine, we have to run today!

ANTOINE. With the frame?

MARIE. Of course.

ANTOINE. And go where?

MARIE. Antoine, I just had a dream that it happened again.

ANTOINE. But it can't.

MARIE. It could.

ANTOINE. Marie, I think you should see one of the portrait counselors again.

MARIE. Customer!

> *(They freeze in the Painting Pose.)*
>
> *(**CUSTOMER 1** up to **ANTOINE.**)*

CUSTOMER 1. Hey, Mister French Metric System, how many inches did they take off your neck?

> *(**CUSTOMER 1** laughs at own joke.)*

*(To **MARIE.**)* And look at you Marie; you're going to be taller than him any minute!

> *(**CUSTOMER 1** laughs and exits.)*

MARIE. Sometimes I want to just reach out and slap them.

ANTOINE. Marie, try to smile.

MARIE. I can't.

ANTOINE. Think of your beautiful dress.

MARIE. Still I cannot smile.

ANTOINE. Oh Marie.

MARIE. 'Cause I keep thinking that Jacques-Louis David knew that in six and a half years you would be named and guillotined.

ANTOINE. How could a painter have known? It's coincidence that I am showing six and a half fingers.

MARIE. CUSTOMER!

> *(They freeze in the Painting Pose.)*
>
> *(**CURATOR** enters.)*

CURATOR. It's just your curator. Don't freak out.

ANTOINE. But the museum's open.

CURATOR. Guards at the doors.

ANTOINE. Are you sure?

CURATOR. 'Cause I just found out about something amazing!

MARIE. Is there something wrong?

CURATOR. Nothing's wrong, Marie. Stop worrying, you're always worrying.

ANTOINE. We were just talking about that.

MARIE. 'Cause I had a dream last night that something terrible happened.

CURATOR. What is going to happen?

ANTOINE. Actually it already happened.

MARIE. May eighth, 1794.

> *(**MARIE** motions as if to cut her neck, then points to **ANTOINE**.)*

CURATOR. Oh that.

MARIE. You know what I'm talking about?

CURATOR. I do, Marie. But please put that out of your mind and think about this, which is really great news.

MARIE. Oh I need really great news!

CURATOR. Quote: "We are hoping that you will allow us to exhibit 'Antoine-Laurent Lavoisier and his Wife' by Jacques-Louis David for a run of six and a half months, in six and a half rooms, opening on June sixth for the first ever 'Back to the Reign of Terror' exhibit at the Louvre Museum in France."

ANTOINE. *(Both hands in the air.)* YES!

MARIE. *(Blood-curdling scream.)* NOOOOOOO!

> *(**MARIE** then faints, falling right on her husband.)*

CURATOR. Is she all right?

ANTOINE. Marie?

MARIE. What?

CURATOR. Is she okay?

ANTOINE. She's okay.

MARIE. Antoine?

ANTOINE. It's okay, Marie. Antoine's here, I'm right here.

MARIE. Antoine, I just had a most terrible dream.

ANTOINE. Open your eyes, Marie.

MARIE. I dreamt that the curator came to us and...

(**MARIE** *sees* **CURATOR.**)

ANTOINE. Marie, it's okay. We can say, "No."

CURATOR. That's right you can say, "No."

MARIE. It's, "No." Absolutely, positively NO!

CURATOR. But before you do, know that you would be reacquainting with old friends.

ANTOINE. Like?

CURATOR. Funny you should ask, you would be with "Ruins of the Tuileries Palace."

(**MARIE** *cries.*)

Is that a good cry?

ANTOINE. Bad.

CURATOR. A drawing of Robespierre.

MARIE. AHHH!

CURATOR. Another bad.

ANTOINE. Not a good list!

CURATOR. Though it's the drawing of the DECAPITATED HEAD of Robespierre.

MARIE & ANTOINE. *(Pause, they smile, applaud.)* OHHH! We like that one!

(**CURATOR** *answers phone.*)

CURATOR. *(Into phone.)* Hello?

(Pause.)

One second.

(To **ANTOINE** *and* **MARIE***.)* It's ELISABETH de FRANCE, Louie the Sixteenth's sister. I have to take this. You talk.

ANTOINE. Good idea.

CURATOR. *(Into phone.)* Liz, I have some great news about an opportunity in France.

> *(***CURATOR*** exits.)*

ANTOINE. Marie.

MARIE. No.

ANTOINE. Come on.

MARIE. Absolutely not.

ANTOINE. To see France.

MARIE. To be captured.

ANTOINE. To be honored.

MARIE. As they hold down our canvas.

ANTOINE. It is the great apology.

MARIE. Cut out your head and throw it into the Seine.

ANTOINE. It is a different France, Marie.

MARIE. My nightmare was right.

ANTOINE. They have a high school named for me.

MARIE. This is why I had the dream.

ANTOINE. Even the Hôtel de Ville has a statue.

MARIE. It is a trap.

ANTOINE. They'll probably put me back at the Academy of Science.

> *(***CURATOR*** enters.)*

MARIE. *(Screams to the heavens.)* I will not. I will not! I WILL NOOOOOOOT!

CURATOR. *(Pause.)* I see you've had a fruitful discussion on the subject.

ANTOINE. We've tossed around a few ideas.

CURATOR. Louie's sister who chose the guillotine is going back!

ANTOINE. Well, we will not go.

MARIE. Thank you, Antoine. But don't be angry.

ANTOINE. But under one condition.

MARIE. Anything.

ANTOINE. That you see one of the portrait counselors again.

MARIE. Uh…

ANTOINE. This week?

MARIE. I will. I promise.

CURATOR. Listen, I uh… I have to chase down David's "The Death of Socrates." I just saw him turn the corner.

> (**CURATOR** *to edge of stage.*)

If you change your mind slip a note under my door.

ANTOINE. Will do.

MARIE. Won't.

ANTOINE. Actually, probably won't.

> (**CURATOR** *smiles, nods, exits.*)

> (**ANTOINE** *exhales, returns to his notes.*)

I'm glad that's over. Now where was I?

> (**MARIE** *over to* **ANTOINE**. *They are back in their Painting Pose.*)

MARIE. Oh Antoine, Antoine, Antoine.

ANTOINE. It does not matter. We are safe, content here.

MARIE. Antoine, yesterday I was reading a French newspaper.

ANTOINE. Now…if I add oxygen.

MARIE. Someone dropped it.

ANTOINE. To the combustion.

MARIE. And it says that in France when one buys a television, the tax office sends you a bill for a television license.

ANTOINE. With these changes.

MARIE. And that the tax office sends you a bill for garbage.

ANTOINE. And ran this experiment.

MARIE. And these are wildly unpopular taxes. So I'm afraid another tax revolution may occur any day, we'd be caught in the middle...

ANTOINE. Customers!

(They strike the Painting Pose.)

CUSTOMER 2. Wait a second. I've heard about this painting.

CUSTOMER 3. Cute couple.

CUSTOMER 2. I think this is the one where he got his head chopped off.

CUSTOMER 3. Did she get her head chopped off?

CUSTOMER 2. No, I think he just got his head chopped.

CUSTOMER 3. So how did this survive?

CUSTOMER 2. Yeah, if this was in France they'd probably have his head cut out.

CUSTOMER 3. Let's go.

CUSTOMER 2. Smart guy staying here.

*(**CUSTOMERS 2** and **3** exit. Pause.)*

MARIE. Did you hear that?

ANTOINE. Yes.

MARIE. Did you hear what he said?

ANTOINE. Sometimes I just want to reach out and slap these people.

*(**MARIE** smiles at **ANTOINE**. **ANTOINE** smiles at **MARIE**. Lights fade. Blackout.)*

Another Misguided Tour

PART III

(Referring to any Audubon print or drawing at the Met.)

WOMAN. Jimmy A. Everybody loves John James Audubon. Haitian, illegitimate son of a French sea captain, who took him to France. Audubon married his neighbor, went bankrupt, went to prison, then went bird hunting while his wife stayed home and worked as a nanny. But what detail! Everyone thinks Audubon was so nice to birds. He killed almost all the birds he painted. He once said, "I call birds few when I shoot less than 100 per day." Then he wired their wings. Put them in a stance. Drew 435 species! Four volumes! That's a lot of dead birds!

(Pause.)

And who can't completely identify with these birds. I mean, after the manicure, pedicure, haircut, makeup, outfit, belt, bag, heels, accessories, all wired to look perfect, don't you feel like that? Flawless, beautiful, yet what movement can we make because of what it cost to look this way? And the cost? Whoa! Last month I spent fifty percent of my salary on product.

(Pause.)

These birds always give me the chills, don't they? I mean, knowing the detail.

(Cheerfully, to tour.) Hey, let's do another, shall we? Follow me!

Another Fertility God Fugue

CHARACTERS

(in order of appearance)

FERTILITY GODS – four actors and actresses posed with percussion instruments

GIORGIO – security guard

MARIA – security guard

SETTING

Bare stage

TIME

Contemporary

*For a list of artwork in this scene, please see the back of the book.

(Lights rise on four **FERTILITY GOD STATUES** *in various poses. The* **FERTILITY GODS** *are actors and actresses wearing masks, costumes, and holding percussion instruments: maracas, drums, finger cymbals, wood blocks, and one with a bass-like string instrument.)*

(Guard **GIORGIO** *enters left, debating to himself.)*

GIORGIO. I should ask her to the dance.

*(***FERTILITY GODS*** begin playing one at a time.)*

Why not?

(Paces right.)

Why can't I ask her to the dance? What is wrong with me?

(Paces left.)

(All **FERTILITY GODS** *begin to gyrate, then dance in unison. They play.)*

When I see her today, I'll just say, "Maria, are you going to the dance, and if so, would you like to go with me?"

(Paces left.)

Why is it so difficult?

(In deep thought, he stands center.)

Then I'll just grab and kiss her and make her want me.

(Pause.)

Not a good idea.

(All **FERTILITY GODS** *freeze.* **GIORGIO** *looks around, clenches fist.)*

I'm doing it now!

(**GIORGIO** *exits stage left, determined.*)

(**FERTILITY GODS** *slap hands in victory.*)

(**MARIA**, *a security guard, enters stage right, debating to herself.*)

MARIA. I should ask him to the dance. Why not? There's nothing wrong with a girl asking a guy to a dance.

(*Paces left.*)

(**FERTILITY GODS** *begin playing one at a time again and this time bass player joins in last and all* **FERTILITY GODS** *begin to gyrate, then dance in unison with overriding bass beat. They play.*)

When I see him today, I'll just say, "Giorgio, are you going to the dance? And then I'll just...freeze like I usually do.

(*Paces right.*)

Why don't I have any confidence?

(*In deep thought, she stands center.*)

Then I'll just throw myself on him and ravage him.

(*Pause.*)

Maybe I should just wait with that.

(*All* **FERTILITY GODS** *freeze.* **MARIA** *looks around, puts hands on both sides of face.*)

If I lose, I lose. I'm doing it!

(**MARIA** *exits stage right, determined.*)

(**FERTILITY GODS** *slap hands in victory.*)

(**GIORGIO** *enters, talking into phone.*)

GIORGIO. I was wondering if Maria is here today? I haven't seen her yet.
Uh-huh, sure, I'll hold.

(**MARIA** *enters, talking into phone.*)

MARIA. I was thinking of asking him, but then I keep thinking.

GIORGIO. She is?

MARIA. *(Noticing* **GIORGIO***.)* Oops, there he is.

GIORGIO. *(Noticing* **MARIA***.)* Oh, there she is.

MARIA. Gotta go.

GIORGIO. Bye.

> (**GIORGIO** *and* **MARIA** *close phones together.)*

FERTILITY GODS. Ohhhh.

GIORGIO. Hi.

MARIA. Hi.

> *(They walk to each other.)*

FERTILITY GODS. Ewweee.

GIORGIO. Can I talk to you for a second?

MARIA. Sure.

FERTILITY GODS. Ahhhh.

GIORGIO. Hey, those are really nice earrings you have there.

MARIA. Oh…thanks. Bought them in the museum shop.

FERTILITY GODS. Mmmmmm.

GIORGIO. Say, there's a uh…a uh.

MARIA. A what?

GIORGIO. A dance? Did you know that there's a dance?

> (**FERTILITY GODS** *begin playing one at a time again, and this time all begin to gyrate, then dance. They play.)*

MARIA. The dinner dance?

GIORGIO. Yes.

MARIA. Here at the museum?

GIORGIO. That's it. That's the one.

MARIA. And it's uh…coming up.

GIORGIO. Yes it is.

> (**GIORGIO** *moves to embrace* **MARIA***. They kiss passionately, then suddenly break back*

> *to their original positions as if nothing happened.)*

MARIA. Hey, are you okay?

GIORGIO. Oh yeah, sorry, there's a lot on my mind today.

MARIA. That's okay. Me, too.

GIORGIO. With all the new regulations we received at last night's meeting.

MARIA. There were a lot, weren't there? But you were saying something about?

GIORGIO. The dance!

MARIA. I was thinking about that this morning too.

GIORGIO. Really? What were you thinking?

MARIA. Well, it's my first year working here, your first year too, right?

GIORGIO. Yup.

MARIA. Well, it seems, it's the event of the year.

GIORGIO. A big deal.

MARIA. Yeah.

GIORGIO. It seems.

MARIA. So when Charlie asked me.

GIORGIO. Charlie?

MARIA. Do you know Charlie?

GIORGIO. No.

MARIA. He works at the main desk?

GIORGIO. I don't like him.

MARIA. I thought you said you didn't know him?

GIORGIO. *(Pause.)* I've heard things.

MARIA. Oh, well…when Charlie asked me to go.

GIORGIO. He did! I mean, he did?

> **(MARIA** *moves to embrace* **GIORGIO.** *They kiss passionately, then suddenly break back to their original positions as if nothing happened.)*

MARIA. Sorry, I seem to have lost my train of.

GIORGIO. You were telling me about Charlie.

MARIA. Oh yeah. Say…is it hot in here?

GIORGIO. It is.

MARIA. They must have turned up the heat.

GIORGIO. I think they did.

FERTILITY GODS.
GETTIN' WARM.

(An **ANNOUNCEMENT** *is heard.)*

ANNOUNCEMENT. ALL GUARDS please take your positions for the museum opening.

MARIA. Gee, we gotta go.

FERTILITY GODS.
GETTIN' HOT.

GIORGIO. Yeah. But what I wanted to talk to you about.

MARIA. Yes.

FERTILITY GODS.
GONNA ASK?

GIORGIO. Was the dance?

MARIA. Really?

FERTILITY GODS.
MAYBE NOT.

GIORGIO. But now that Charlie.

MARIA. I'm not going with Charlie.

FERTILITY GODS.
WANT TO HUG.

GIORGIO. Oh.

MARIA. I told Charlie, "No."

GIORGIO. Oh.

FERTILITY GODS.
WANT TO KISS.

MARIA. A big, "No."

GIORGIO. OOOKay.

FERTILITY GODS.
WANT TO LOSE.

MARIA. So I'm not going with anyone right now. No one. Not anyone at all, in case you're wondering. Just to set that straight.

GIORGIO. I'm not either.

FERTILITY GODS.

ANOTHER MISS.

MARIA. Uh-huh.

GIORGIO. So uh.

FERTILITY GODS. Take a stand!

MARIA. Well, if you're not going with anyone.

GIORGIO. And you're not going with anyone.

*(**FERTILITY GODS** stop playing.)*

FERTILITY GODS. Ask!

MARIA. UMMM...

GIORGIO. Uhhh...

FERTILITY GODS. For the love of all the gods, ASK!

(They both move to embrace, they kiss passionately, then suddenly break back to their original positions as if nothing happened.)

GIORGIO & MARIA. What was I just thinking? Oh, would you like to go to the Museum Dinner Dance with me?

(Pause.)

Did you just ask me to go to the dance?

(Pause.)

Did we just say the same thing?

(Pause.)

FERTILITY GODS. Gasp.

GIORGIO & MARIA. Whoa!

FERTILITY GODS. Yeah!

GIORGIO & MARIA. Soooo?

FERTILITY GODS. WELL?

GIORGIO & MARIA. Sure.

*(**FERTILITY GODS** applaud.)*

I'd love...to go.

*(**GIORGIO** and **MARIA** back away.)*

I better get back to my spot.

(Back away some more.)

Talk to you.

(More.)

Okay.

(More.)

Soon.

(More.)

Later.

(Stop before exit and to themselves.)

That was the weirdest thing that ever.

*(Lights begin to fade. **GIORGIO** and **MARIA** exit. **FERTILITY GODS** break into frenzy and play. Then freeze. Blackout.)*

Intermission

Broken Eggs

CHARACTERS

(in order of appearance)

CYNTHIA – female

VOICE – male or female, a voice-over

SETTING

Bare stage, frame, chair

TIME

Contemporary

*For a list of artwork in this scene, please see the back of the book.

(Lights rise on an actress. Sitting on a stool.)

VOICE. Cynthia?

CYNTHIA. Yes?

VOICE. Break's almost over.

CYNTHIA. I know.

VOICE. Gotta head back.

CYNTHIA. I will.

VOICE. With the basket and the broken eggs.

CYNTHIA. Yup.

VOICE. And don't leave any eggs behind.

CYNTHIA. Nope.

VOICE. By the way, on break could you not take the basket with you?

CYNTHIA. I thought I had to take the basket?

VOICE. It's museum policy not to take items that aren't attached.

CYNTHIA. But they say the eggs and basket are a part of me.

VOICE. Don't we believe everything we read in the guidebook.

CYNTHIA. Actually I'd like to leave the basket there.

VOICE. And Cynthia, I think we may have a bit of a situation here.

CYNTHIA. I still have five minutes left.

VOICE. Yes, yes you do. But you're on the stage they use for lectures and I think some people are coming in.

CYNTHIA. So?

VOICE. I just don't want you to be in an embarrassing situation.

CYNTHIA. More embarrassing than my painting?

VOICE. Cynthia, I think an audience is forming.

CYNTHIA. *(Stands.)* Yeah, you're right.

VOICE. It'll take three or four minutes to get back from here.

CYNTHIA. *(Crossing apron, enthused.)* An audience.

VOICE. So let's head out.

CYNTHIA. Hello?

VOICE. Cynthia, that's against the rules.

CYNTHIA. How are you today?

VOICE. Cynthia?

CYNTHIA. And hello back there.

VOICE. If you don't leave now, you won't make it back.

CYNTHIA. Hi.

VOICE. Let's not do this.

CYNTHIA. No, I'm going to do this. I have some things to say.

(Three beeps are heard.)

VOICE. Hello. Uh...I have a small announcement for those coming into the lecture: the lecture has been moved across the hall to a bigger and better venue.

CYNTHIA. Why's that?

VOICE. I don't know. But, if you will now exit, and move directly across the hall.

CYNTHIA. Unless you'd like to hear me.

VOICE. Cynthia, there's nothing that you can say that will interest them.

CYNTHIA. Au contraire, my friend.

VOICE. Ladies and gentlemen, we are going to be shutting off the lights in this lecture hall in approximately five minutes.

CYNTHIA. Not true.

VOICE. Cynthia, remember if you're late getting back, your mother will be very upset.

CYNTHIA. So what's she going to do, scream at me like she's already doing in the picture?

VOICE. Cynthia, something's wrong. What's wrong? Can you tell me?

CYNTHIA. Yes, I'll tell you what's wrong. Do you know what day it is?

VOICE. Well, I know it's your anniversary.

CYNTHIA. Yes it is. It's been two hundred and fifty-seven years and today my lover gives me this.

(**CYNTHIA** *holds up something small.*)

VOICE. A ring?

CYNTHIA. A ring!

VOICE. An Engagement Ring?

CYNTHIA. He says a Pre-Engagement Friendship Ring.

VOICE. After two hundred and fifty-seven years?

CYNTHIA. He's a slow mover.

VOICE. That's for sure.

CYNTHIA. But a ring! And a move toward a commitment!

VOICE. Cynthia, you know that you can't wear that.

CYNTHIA. Why not?

VOICE. No ring.

CYNTHIA. Please?

VOICE. How can you? Think of your brother, your mother, your composition.

CYNTHIA. I want a ring.

VOICE. It would ruin everything. You and your lover, mother and brother would be taken off the wall and no one would want to see you.

CYNTHIA. Oh boo-hoo.

VOICE. 'Cause you and your lover would make no sense together.

CYNTHIA. That's a very mean thing to say.

VOICE. It's true.

CYNTHIA. I just want a different life. I don't want to be "that" woman anymore.

VOICE. Cynthia, think how lucky you are to be the focus of a famous painting.

CYNTHIA. That's easy for you to say. You don't have all the tour guides and young girls pointing at you shaking their heads. The point is, I depress people. And after 257 years, I think it's finally gotten to me too.

VOICE. Cynthia.

CYNTHIA. It's not fair.

VOICE. No, it's not.

CYNTHIA. Most women in paintings are adored.

VOICE. But it beats the alternative.

CYNTHIA. Which is?

VOICE. Not existing. Painted over. Pushed against each other in storage. You think your lover likes holding your mother back, she likes screaming? And your little brother likes trying to put that egg together all these years, that poor little kid.

CYNTHIA. I could keep the ring in my pocket.

VOICE. Actually you could, but...

CYNTHIA. I could?

VOICE. But it wouldn't change how people view you.

CYNTHIA. It would change how *I* view me.

VOICE. Let's think about it.

CYNTHIA. I'd like that.

VOICE. Why don't we go back, we'll talk about it.

CYNTHIA. Really?

VOICE. Yes.

CYNTHIA. If we can talk about it.

VOICE. Absolutely.

CYNTHIA. *(Smiles toward audience.)* Two hundred and fifty-seven years and finally a "maybe."

(**CYNTHIA** *picks up basket.*)

VOICE. Let's go, broken eggs.

CYNTHIA. That's future, *MRS.* Broken Eggs to you.

(**CYNTHIA** *turns, exits.*)

(*Lights fade. Blackout.*)

Another Misguided Tour

PART IV

(Referring to Thomas Cole's "View from Mount Holyoke, Northampton, Massachusetts, after a Thunderstorm.")

WOMAN. The father of the Hudson River School, Thomas Cole, moved to America at seventeen, and he and his pupil Frederic Edwin Church were the most influential landscape painters. This is: "View from Mount Holyoke, Massachusetts." On the right a beautiful day, on the left, a thunderstorm. In the middle bottom of the painting, Thomas Cole painted himself painting this painting. Is this not like life? Thinking all is well when in reality a raging tempest is bearing down? I can completely identify with this. Who knows what torrential downpour is behind us? Who knew after putting Ted through law school that three days after graduation Ted would tell me that he was leaving me for a ten-year-older woman with a seat on the stock exchange. Who could have seen that coming? So this painting means a lot, not only as a warning, but as a reminder. Hey, enough storm clouds. Let's just move on, shall we?

Here Sphinxie, Sphinxie!

(or Sphinxes, Femme Fatales, and Apples!)

CHARACTERS

(in order of appearance)

ARISTOTLE – male or female

SPHINX – only head and part of wings visible

MAES – female

POLICE – offstage voice

SETTING

Bare stage, small partition, one chair

TIME

Contemporary

*For a list of artwork in this scene, please see the back of the book.

Winner! 2016 Goshen College Peace Award

(Lights rise on chair downstage left and a four-foot-high partition that extends upstage the entire length of the upstage. There is also a window upstage right, which can just be the wings. It is midnight and lights are half-normal and about enough to see.)

*(**ARISTOTLE** enters as if calling a cat and crosses left to center. He carries a flashlight but doesn't need it.)*

ARISTOTLE. Here kitty, kitty. Here kitty.

*(**SPHINX**'s head peers over counter and hisses. We only see **SPHINX**'s woman's face and tiara and the top of her wings looking over the counter. **SPHINX** then goes back down.)*

Here Sphinxie, Sphinxie. Where are you, Sphinxie?

*(**ARISTOTLE** crosses from center and exits stage right.)*

*(**SPHINX** rises and hisses again.)*

*(**MAES** enters, sits in chair, and begins to peel apple.)*

MAES. I know you're here. And I'm going to sit here till you want to talk to me.

SPHINX. I'm going to jump.

MAES. No you're not.

SPHINX. Out that window.

MAES. Have you looked out that window?

*(**SPHINX** hisses out window.)*

SPHINX. Who called them?

POLICE. *(Offstage voice.)* Please move away from the window.

SPHINX. Maes, did you call them?

MAES. When you opened the window, you activated the alarm.

> (**SPHINX** *again to window. A bright light comes on from offstage.*)

POLICE. *(Offstage voice.)* If you jump, we have a net.

SPHINX. They have a net.

MAES. Almost makes you want to jump.

SPHINX. They're making me crazy.

MAES. Calm down. You're getting yourself all worked up.

SPHINX. That's easy for you to say.

> (**ARISTOTLE** *enters from stage right.*)

ARISTOTLE. Here Sphinxie, Sphinxie.

> (**ARISTOTLE** *stops, whispers to* **MAES**.)

PSST.

MAES. What?

ARISTOTLE. She's in here.

MAES. Why do think I'm sitting here?

ARISTOTLE. We have to close the window.

MAES. You try and she'll fly.

ARISTOTLE. Can she fly?

MAES. And she'll hurt herself.

ARISTOTLE. You get her away from the window, I'll close it.

MAES. No.

ARISTOTLE. If we work as a team.

MAES. Not a team player.

ARISTOTLE. But Maes.

MAES. Aristotle, I peel apples alone in my painting, I've always been alone, she's my only friend.

ARISTOTLE. But as our union rep.

MAES. Not impressed.

ARISTOTLE. This action of hers will jeopardize any of us from ever going for walks in the park.

MAES. C'est la vie.

ARISTOTLE. That's very selfish.

MAES. Want an apple?

ARISTOTLE. Maes, down that hallway waits an entire SWAT team with nets and tranquilizing guns.

MAES. *(Looks around, waves.)* Anyone else want an apple?

> (**MAES** *smiles at* **ARISTOTLE**, *then back to peeling.)*

ARISTOTLE. How can someone like you who represents such modesty and peace, be friends with such a man-hating beast?

MAES. She's just so funny.

ARISTOTLE. So you're not going to help?

MAES. For instance, my painting is called: "Young Woman Peeling Apples," she calls it: "Babe With a Blade."

ARISTOTLE. On the other hand, when you want to go out for a walk in the park, who stands up for you?

MAES. Aristotle, you're a good guy, I'm not.

ARISTOTLE. I did not say that.

MAES. And she's even worse.

ARISTOTLE. Hey, remember last year when this sphinx went on the roof, what happened?

MAES. I do.

ARISTOTLE. They tranquilized her down?

MAES. That was terrible.

ARISTOTLE. Then locked us down for a month. No roof garden at night, no windows on Monday, no park privileges.

MAES. Okay.

ARISTOTLE. Sit in your isolated world, Maes, have fun with your man-hating friend, but when we lose, don't come crying to me.

MAES. Okay, I understand.

ARISTOTLE. I am going to talk to them, find out what they want me to do, then I am coming back and I hope you will help.

MAES. I'll think about it.

ARISTOTLE. Be right back with a plan.

MAES. Aristotle?

ARISTOTLE. What?

MAES. Her name is not "man-hating beast" or "Sphinx" it's Cleo.

ARISTOTLE. I'll be right back.

> (*As* **ARISTOTLE** *exits,* **SPHINX** *raises her head and hisses.*)

SPHINX. (*Making fun of how* **ARISTOTLE** *speaks.*) You're such an idiot; you're going to ruin it for all of us.

MAES. He's right; you're going to get shot again.

SPHINX. Not if I fly higher.

MAES. Oh yeah? And where are you going?

SPHINX. The Madison Square Garden building.

MAES. Are you kidding?

SPHINX. I've thought about it a long time.

MAES. It's forty blocks away.

SPHINX. I was talking to Diana about the building. Do you know her?

MAES. Who?

SPHINX. Gold nude goddess, American wing sculpture, has a bow and arrow.

MAES. Oh, Diana.

SPHINX. Beautiful woman, slender.

MAES. I know Diana.

SPHINX. She's modeled after some guy's mistress who was building Madison Square Garden.

MAES. She's nuts.

SPHINX. She is.

MAES. She shot another tour director today.

SPHINX. Good for her. I hate 'em too.

MAES. Grazed the lady's butt. They may put safety tips on her.

SPHINX. Well, she was on top, says the view is gorgeous.

MAES. Cleo, they'll take away a lot of privileges.

SPHINX. I'll negotiate before I come down. So, you turn off the lights when I say, "Ready on three."

MAES. Cleo, why are you all frustrated? You don't get like this unless someone did something to you.

SPHINX. I don't want to talk about it.

MAES. Who was it?

SPHINX. It's none of your business.

MAES. It is my business. I'm your friend.

SPHINX. Never mind.

MAES. What did they do Cleo?

SPHINX. Nothing.

MAES. Oh I know...someone answered that new riddle of yours, didn't they?

SPHINX. Maybe.

MAES. Was it Oedipus?

SPHINX. Nope.

MAES. That Rodin uh... What's that statue?

SPHINX. "The Thinker."

MAES. "The Thinker"?

SPHINX. Nope.

MAES. Will you please help me help you?

SPHINX. It was Aristotle.

(**MAES** *gasps.*)

In front of everyone.

MAES. Why didn't you tell me?

SPHINX. So embarrassing. I don't want to go back to European Painting, I just want out!

MAES. Okay Cleo, this has happened before with riddles. So let's first try to put this in perspective.

(**ARISTOTLE** *enters, calling with flashlight.*)

ARISTOTLE. Here Sphinxie, Sphinxie...

MAES. You answered her riddle?

ARISTOTLE. What?

MAES. You know how she reacts to people, especially men, answering her riddles.

ARISTOTLE. I know.

MAES. What is wrong with you?

ARISTOTLE. I'm sorry.

MAES. A man of learning, harassing a poor psychotic man-hating hybrid?

ARISTOTLE. *(Whispers.)* I don't like her.

MAES. I am shocked.

ARISTOTLE. She prances around the sculpture court.

MAES. Oh let her be.

ARISTOTLE. With that tiara.

MAES. Oh please.

ARISTOTLE. She was berating Ugolino. Solve this riddle: "There are two sisters: one gives birth to the other...and she, in turn, gives birth to the first." Poor Ugolino, he is starving to death with his sons and grandsons. Why is she taunting them?

SPHINX. And he answered it.

ARISTOTLE. I apologized three times.

SPHINX. Screams out the answer.

ARISTOTLE. There is just so much a man can take.

SPHINX. "Night and Day," it's "Night and Day," that gives birth to each other.

ARISTOTLE. If I need to apologize again to close the window, I will.

SPHINX. Everyone: Oedipus, Adam, Perseus, even the head of Medusa was laughing, "Night and Day, Day and Night." That's why Maes, I am ready on three.

MAES. *(To* **ARISTOTLE.***)* You should be ashamed of yourself.

ARISTOTLE. She's so pushy.

MAES. To be the cause of this.

ARISTOTLE. It was in the moment.

MAES. Allowing passion to escalate a violent situation?

ARISTOTLE. Maes, if this gets out, I'll lose the upcoming election.

MAES. You deserve to lose the upcoming election.

ARISTOTLE. You have to help me, Maes.

MAES. Then I'm going to tell you what we're going to do.

ARISTOTLE. Well, they have a plan.

MAES. Never mind their plan. This is what you are going to do.

ARISTOTLE. But MAES.

MAES. You are going to call off the museum SWAT team and shut that light off.

ARISTOTLE. I can't tell them what to do.

MAES. Yes you can. You are going to close the spotlights for one minute and I will close the window.

ARISTOTLE. How?

MAES. I don't know how. Never mind how. Just shut down the lights, I'll close the window.

ARISTOTLE. Okay.

MAES. Do you understand?

ARISTOTLE. I do.

MAES. Now go.

ARISTOTLE. Thanks, Maes.

MAES. Don't thank me, it may not work.

ARISTOTLE. No wonder everyone loves your painting, you're so serene, so calm.

MAES. Now go! Call off your SWAT team and maybe you'll win your election. Oh, Father of reason and logic.

ARISTOTLE. I am, I am. Good luck!

> *(***ARISTOTLE*** *exits.)*

> *(***SPHINX*** *hisses at* ***ARISTOTLE*** *and then out the window.)*

POLICE. *(Offstage.)* Move away from the window! We have weapons pointed!

(MAES stands.)

MAES. Cleo?

(SPHINX looks at MAES.)

This beautiful apple says: "To the Fairest!"

(SPHINX smiles.)

Like the apple that started the Trojan War, the fall of Eden.

(SPHINX smile and nods.)

Cleo loves apples, doesn't she?

(SPHINX nods.)

Cleo wants apple, doesn't she?

(SPHINX nods.)

Sit.

(SPHINX sits so we can barely see her.)

(MAES crosses upstage to near partition.)

Beg.

(SPHINX begs so we can see her head and wings.)

(MAES gives SPHINX apple. Perhaps puts it on counter so we can see SPHINX licking and taking small bites out and purring. Perhaps MAES pets SPHINX. SPHINX rubs head against hand as cats react to petting. Ask a cat lover for details.)

(Light goes out from wings. MAES closes or exits and we hear window close. MAES enters.)

Good Cleo.

SPHINX. Good apple.

MAES. Good girl.

(MAES crosses to chair.)

SPHINX. Hmmm.

MAES. Cleo, nobody understands you like I do.

SPHINX. Yum, yum, yum. Yum.

MAES. And nobody understands apples like we do.

    *(**MAES** sits, peeling another apple.)*

SPHINX. Cleo loves apples.

MAES. Yes.

SPHINX. Maes peels perfect apples.

MAES. Yes.

SPHINX. Cleo loves Maes.

MAES. And everybody thinks Aristotle is the Father of Logic. Baa!

    *(**MAES** laughs.)*

SPHINX. BAaa!

    *(**MAES** laughs, **SPHINX** laughs with **MAES**.)*

SPHINX & MAES. BAAAaaa!

    (They laugh.)

    *(**ARISTOTLE** enters, running to **MAES**, whispers:)*

ARISTOTLE. They're gone. Everything's secure. Thank you.

MAES. You're welcome.

ARISTOTLE. You're a genius dealing with this man-hating sexual deviant.

MAES. Don't mention it.

ARISTOTLE. And if I may say so. You look very cute today.

MAES. Who's the deviant? I'm fifteen.

ARISTOTLE. Actually, you're over three hundred and fifty years old.

MAES. Go away.

ARISTOTLE. May I have an apple?

    *(**MAES** gives **ARISTOTLE** apple.)*

Thanks.

    *(**ARISTOTLE** exits.)*

MAES. And they wonder why I carry a knife?

(**MAES** *hisses at* **ARISTOTLE**. **SPHINX** *looks up, hisses too.*)

MAES. Yeah, you tell him.

(*Lights fade. Blackout.*)

Another Misguided Tour

PART V

*(Referring to Jean-Baptiste-Siméon Chardin's
"The Silver Tureen.")*

WOMAN. Still life. Or tables full of fruit and vegetables. The
only thing never original about still life are the titles:
"Still Life," "Still Life with Fruit," "Still Life with Lobster
and Fruit." This, my favorite: "The Silver Tureen," Jean-
Baptiste-Siméon Chardin, 1728. See the cat crouching
about to pounce on the dead rabbit? Any young
woman can completely identify with that in this city.
If you are not being hit on by some twenty-something
with something to prove, you are being hit on by some
fifty-something divorcée with something to prove.
Either way you feel cooked or hunted. By the way, this
is famous 'cause it blends the emotions of cooking and
hunting. Hey, let's speed up, shall we, 'cause I have a
very important third date, and I'm supposed to be in
a Second Avenue restaurant in about thirty minutes.
Hey, we only have one more to go anyway, and so what
do you say we move a little quicker? Come on, let's
move it! Keep up!

The Art of Detention

CHARACTERS
(in order of appearance)

BABY MAES – female, from the painting "The Lacemaker"
CHARDIN – male, from the painting "Soap Bubbles"
DIANA – female, Saint-Gauden's American sculpture
GUARD – male

SETTING

Bare stage, folding chairs with top to write on and one high chair that
an actress can hide behind and only show her head and arms
in a baby costume

TIME

Contemporary

*For a list of artwork in this scene, please see the back of the book.

*(Lights rise on **BABY MAES** laughing, throwing sippy cup up in air, and catching it yelling, "WHOA!" A man [**CHARDIN**] laughing while blowing bubbles and a woman [**DIANA**] dressed in gold clothes and face also laughing making believe she is shooting the bubbles with an arrow. She has a bow in her hand. A bell sounds. **GUARD** enters and stands there like a teacher entering a detention out of control.)*

GUARD. All right, listen up.

(They don't.)

I said, "Attention."

*(They don't care. **GUARD** takes out clipboard, turns paper.)*

Diana, nude sculpture, American wing?

(Pause.)

If I don't hear from you, you're not here.

(They don't care.)

I said: "If I don't hear from you, you're not here."

*(**DIANA** stops.)*

DIANA. What happens then?

GUARD. Then you stay here till we hear from you.

DIANA. Here.

GUARD. Thank you.

(Turns paper on clipboard.)

"Soap Bubbles," Jean-Baptiste-Siméon Chardin, European wing?

CHARDIN. Does it look like I'm here?

GUARD. Chardin, cut the attitude, do your work and you'll be out of here.

CHARDIN. Repression, repression!

GUARD. Baby Maes, "The Lacemaker," European wing?

BABY MAES. Over here, very upset and I might need a changing soon. *(Laughs.)*

GUARD. You mean, a change of attitude.

ALL. Ohhhhhh!

BABY MAES. And a wipe. I may need a wipe. You gonna do it big guy?

GUARD. All right. You know the rules. You've all been here before. There's extra paper, pencils here.
(Reading.) Diana: 500 times, "I will not shoot tour directors."

> *(Turns page.)*

Chardin: 500 times, "I will not blow bubbles."

> *(Turns page.)*

Baby Maes: 500, "I will not throw sippy cup."

> *(Looks up.)*

Ball's in your court. I'm leaving at the end of this. But will you?

> *(**GUARD** sits. **CHARDIN** sits. **BABY MAES** is quiet. **DIANA** up to **GUARD**.)*

DIANA. Johnny, Johnny, Johnny.

GUARD. That does you no good.

DIANA. Talk to me.

GUARD. Nothing to talk about.

DIANA. *(Running fingers through* **GUARD**'s *hair.)* Look at your hair. Real hair.

GUARD. I wish you wouldn't do that.

DIANA. Do you like me?

GUARD. I think you are very nice. Yes?

DIANA. As a woman? Do you like me?

YOU MAKE MY FRAME SHAKE!

GUARD. I think you're a very nice woman? Yes.

DIANA. If it were Friday night, roof garden soirée, would you, as they say, "hit on me"? Buy me a drink, Johnny?

GUARD. Listen, you have a lot of work to do. And I would do it.

CHARDIN. Or would you hit on me, Johnny?

GUARD. Why don't we all do our work.

BABY MAES. Or me! Maybe he'd hit on me and get arrested!

GUARD. And Baby Maes, this is twice this month we meet.

BABY MAES. First: It's Master Maes. And this one was not my fault.

GUARD. Never is, right?

BABY MAES. It was a selfie stick. The couple were swinging a selfie stick. It was coming right at my mother. I hit him right in back of the head with the cup, he dropped the stick.

GUARD. Really?

BABY MAES. Yeah! I love my mother. I'm going to let my mother be hit?

DIANA. Good for you.

(DIANA and CHARDIN clap. GUARD joins in.)

BABY MAES. That's what I said.

CHARDIN. Here, here!

GUARD. They are out of control with those sticks. Yesterday, I broke up a duel in Arms and Armor. Two guys fighting over who was first at a Samurai exhibit.

CHARDIN. One time one went right by my face. She was carrying it like a fishing pole.

GUARD. They're illegal but.

DIANA. They still pull them out.

GUARD. They're not supposed to.

CHARDIN. You should put the customers in detention.

BABY MAES. But yet, I'm in detention.

GUARD. I have no control over that.

DIANA. I know Johnny, you're a good guy. You're just doing what THE MAN tells you to do.

GUARD. Did you appeal?

BABY MAES. No.

GUARD. Why not?

DIANA. I did.

CHARDIN. I did too.

BABY MAES. It's the nineteenth time I've thrown.

DIANA. In three hundred and fifty-nine years? That's nothing.

BABY MAES. This year.

DIANA. OH!

CHARDIN. Oh wow.

GUARD. Really?

DIANA. You are out of control, babe.

BABY MAES. Don't call me babe. I'm older than you.

DIANA. Pardon me.

BABY MAES. I don't like that, "babe." I'm not a babe.

CHARDIN. Touchy, touchy.

GUARD. Okay, why don't we start what we have to do. Does everyone have paper?

DIANA. Johnny, I have to ask you. Do you like tour directors?

GUARD. Yeah, they're okay. Without them half the people wouldn't be here.

CHARDIN. That would be fine with me.

BABY MAES. That'd be great.

DIANA. I hate 'em. I hate 'em all. I'd like to take an arrow and shoot every one of those bastards right through the heart.

ALL. (*Except* **DIANA.**) Whoaaaa!

BABY MAES. Tell it like it is, Diana!

DIANA. How would you like people pointing at you every minute of every day, making fun of you?

GUARD. Diana, I know where you're going with this. We've been through this. It's not going to change.

DIANA. If I were in storage it would.

GUARD. That's the goal?

DIANA. Maybe.

BABY MAES. She shot three tour directors this week.

GUARD. That could do it.

CHARDIN. I'm shocked you're not.

DIANA. Or higher, I want to be way up so I can't hear them. "She is the mistress of the architect of Madison Square Garden," and on and on. It was love. He loved me!

BABY MAES. Is it true about the rubber tips?

DIANA. How'd you hear that?

BABY MAES. I hear everything.

CHARDIN. Is that true?

BABY MAES. They might put them on your arrows?

DIANA. I will shoot them immediately.

CHARDIN. I'm just blowing bubbles and they threw me in here with these psychotics.

DIANA. I am not a psychotic! And if I am, they made me a psychotic.

GUARD. Okay. Okay. I think we've had enough discussion on our problems. We are not going to solve anything here.

CHARDIN. But it's good to talk about it.

GUARD. Sometimes.

DIANA. Always.

GUARD. You do know that we have counselors available twenty-four-seven.

DIANA. I don't like them. I like you Johnny. You listen. The guards listen.

GUARD. But I don't know how to help. They know how to help.

DIANA. Yes with safety tips and 500-sentence punishments?

GUARD. That's not the counselors, that's the disciplinary board. You have to get that straight.

DIANA. Why don't they work together?

GUARD. I don't know. This is beyond me.

BABY MAES. You tell them for us, Johnny.

GUARD. I'm just a guard.

CHARDIN. I am blowing bubbles. Listen to this. I am on my break. My break, mind you! In a lecture hall, blowing bubbles. Some customers come in and I thought, "Hey, this is my time, my space, I'm blowing my bubbles." The bubbles I love, I adore, I worship. So the customers sit. They're watching. They ask some question. I explain. I'm blowing larger ones, larger ones. They begin to cheer. Suddenly I hear:

> (*Lights change to spot on* **CHARDIN.** *We are in the lecture hall story* **CHARDIN** *is telling.*)

VOICE. Chardin? I have a security question.

CHARDIN. Yes.

VOICE. What are you doing?

CHARDIN. Hanging out.

VOICE. Did you set this up?

CHARDIN. I'm on break.

VOICE. I thought we talked about this?

CHARDIN. We did.

VOICE. I thought we reached an agreement about this.

CHARDIN. Listen, they came in.

VOICE. You're not supposed to talk to people, you're a painting.

CHARDIN. Sorry.

VOICE. The problem, Chardin, is that your break has now become a performance.

CHARDIN. But let me explain.

VOICE. We're a museum, not a sideshow.

CHARDIN. But they had questions. And I explained.

VOICE. Chardin, paintings don't explain. A painting like your bubble just "is." Remember we talked about just "Be the Bubble"?

CHARDIN. My bubble is important.

VOICE. Yes it is, Chardin.

CHARDIN. Don't make fun.

VOICE. I'm not making fun.

CHARDIN. You're demeaning my bubble.

VOICE. I'm not demeaning your bubble.

CHARDIN. I see what you're doing?

VOICE. I'm just trying to put it into perspective.

CHARDIN. This is just another way to discourage me.

VOICE. No, I'm not.

CHARDIN. Put me down.

VOICE. I'm not putting you down, Chardin.

CHARDIN. Maybe I'm a slight image of just a man blowing a solitary bubble.

VOICE. Chardin, we all appreciate you.

(Spot off. Lights change back to present scene.)

CHARDIN. And that's when I lost it.

DIANA. What'd you do?

CHARDIN. I pulled out the gun.

GUARD, DIANA & BABY MAES. What?

GUARD. A gun?

DIANA. Chardin!

CHARDIN. Yeah.

BABY MAES. Oh my lord!

CHARDIN. And I let it rip.

*(**CHARDIN** pulls out bubble gun and, laughing wildly, lets it rip, running around apron over audience.)*

"Be the bubble"? There's your bubble baby!

(They all laugh, applaud, cheer.)

You be the bubble! See how it feels to be the bubble! I've been the Bubble. I am the Bubble. See what it's like to blow bubbles over two hundred and eighty years with no damm appreciation!

GUARD. Wow!

BABY MAES. Yes!

DIANA. You go Chardin!

CHARDIN. There were bubbles everywhere. Covered the place. They had to close the lecture hall. It looked like a laundromat exploded. I was off the wall like that.

GUARD. Where did you get that?

BABY MAES. Can you get me one?

CHARDIN. Some kids forgot them in the coatroom. This is the second one. Genius idea. Invention of the millennium. And you better not say anything.

GUARD. I didn't hear anything you just said.

CHARDIN. Johnny, you're okay.

DIANA. *(Runs her hands through* **GUARD***'s hair.)* Isn't he the best?

GUARD. Okay, enough with the hair. Have a seat.

> **(DIANA** *does.)*

Now listen. Chardin, I'm sorry they pushed you like that.

CHARDIN. AH!

GUARD. They shouldn't have pushed you like that.

> **(CHARDIN** *sits.)*

CHARDIN. Forget it. I was a hundred years overdue for an explosion.

GUARD. *(To* **DIANA***.)* And the tour guides should be nicer.

DIANA. "Why? It's true," they say, "I'm just doing my job."

GUARD. Because we should work together.

DIANA. I appreciate that, Johnny.

GUARD. *(To* **BABY MAES***.)* And we're trying to crack down on the selfie sticks. We had a big meeting yesterday.

BABY MAES. *(Sarcastically.)* Good luck with that!

GUARD. But thinking about it. There is something I can do about your situation today.

CHARDIN. What?

DIANA. What do you mean?

BABY MAES. What are you talking about?

GUARD. Well, if. And this better not go any further than this room.

CHARDIN, DIANA & BABY MAES. Nooooo. What? What?

GUARD. Well, if. If you fill out one side of the paper, which I think is twenty-five lines. Am I right?

CHARDIN. Yeah.

DIANA. Right.

BABY MAES. It is.

GUARD. Then I could, maybe, if everybody cooperates…I could run down to the color copier in Drawing and Prints and make.

BABY MAES. Twenty copies!

GUARD. Is that right?

BABY MAES. Twenty-five lines, twenty copies equals 500.

DIANA. All right Baby Maes.

BABY MAES. What did you say?

DIANA. Okay. What do they call you?

BABY MAES. Master Maes.

DIANA. Then… All right, Master Maes!

BABY MAES. Thank you.

GUARD. But you have to do the twenty-five lines.

CHARDIN. I will.

DIANA. I'm doing it!

BABY MAES. I'm on this!

GUARD. And legible.

CHARDIN. Make them clear.

DIANA. Try to make them all the same.

BABY MAES. What an idea. Genius.

GUARD. And you'll be back on the wall. On your base. With your mom tomorrow.

    (It is quiet. They are all writing.)

There we go. Everybody's working. Everybody's happy.

    (**GUARD** *sits.*)

GUARD. And I can read.

DIANA. What are you reading Johnny?

GUARD. I am reading, The Art of Detention.

(Lights fade. Blackout.)

Thought – A Love Story

.

CHARACTERS

THE THINKER – male or female

SETTING

Bare stage, chair

TIME

Present

*For a list of artwork in this scene, please see the back of the book.

(Lights rise on Rodin's **THE THINKER.***)*

THE THINKER. Imagine yourself a frozen nude...up on a shelf...looking down on humanity.

*(***THE THINKER*** rises, moves to center of apron.)*

It's hard to contemplate 'cause who wants to be frozen, unable to move? But I don't mean that in a bad way, like you're trapped, but rather like it's a game you're playing. So it's kind of cool, isn't it? Granted, you can't move, and that's what's so scary, 'cause if you did, then they'd take you off of the shelf, melt you down and you could end up in Abstract as a bolt or a bicycle wheel spinning backward. And who'd want that? That's helpless. That's crazy. That's something you don't want to think about. Spinning forever. All those faces, smiles elongated, out of proportion, due to the fact that you're moving and they're moving, like two side-by-side trains unsure which is actually in motion. When you both are! Whew! Forget that thought! I'd rather be frozen. At least you're still taking it in, contemplating the humanity below you, like a king. Though you're nude. There aren't many nude kings. Which has always bothered me. I mean, I understand the concept. The concept's clear. But it gets drafty up here. And then that's all you're thinking, "Why is it so drafty? Why'd they put me up here near the air conditioning ducts where it's like...sixty degrees eternally?" And seeing, or so the story goes, I'm supposed to be over the Gates of Hell, where one would assume it's hot. I mean, isn't that a valid assumption for the daily weather forecast for that region? "Let's go to the map, Dante. It's hot today, with a probable chance for more heat!" I mean, isn't that a probable assumption? But no, it's drafty. Which was puzzling for the first couple decades, till I figured that out.

(Pause.)

I'm probably boring you, aren't I? You're probably thinking, "He's so boring. He looks cool. Looking down on me. Contemplating it all, like some Pantheon god. Ruling thought. An archetype to be reckoned with." But then doesn't the boring thought just kind of slip in sideways and you say, "All right, I've seen it. That's the guy thinking. Got a picture. Been there, thought that! I'm bored. He's boring. And why is it so drafty here? Near this boring nude guy up there contemplating whatever the hell he is thinking about?"

(He returns to his place, sits in Thinker pose. He takes a deep breath, exhales.)

I love thinking. And there's a lot to think about.

(Pause.)

There's really...really a lot to think about!

(Lights fade. Blackout.)

Another Misguided Tour

PART VI

(Referring to George Bingham's "Fur Traders Descending the Missouri.")

WOMAN. Which finally finds us in conclusion with George Caleb Bingham. Genius. So famous. "Fur Traders Descending the Missouri." See the leashed bear cub on the front of the boat? It looks like a cat but supposed to be a bear cub. Don't you feel like that? You are on a journey, you're on a short leash there on the front of the boat. You know you're moving, you know you're going somewhere, but you don't know who's steering? You're just floating along doing your thing, yet, there's a bit of desperation in the calmness? And you feel real independent out there, but when you turn around you always realize that you've given some guy in your life the paddle. As a side note, George Bingham was an unsuccessful portrait painter who decided that he would just paint local rough tough Missouri boatmen, who now aren't around anymore. Waa-la. Cha-Ching! Remember that: Paint things that aren't going to be around much longer! When I was in college I always painted my boyfriends. And if I had continued that with my internship here at the museum since Ted left me, I'd have a whole gallery. Hell, I'd have a cyclorama!

(Pause.)

Hey, so to wrap up Nature and Landscape's three big rules:

Use contrasts, details and anything not going to be around long. All these artists followed that, and though bankrupt and complete failures, they all created masterpieces! They all got lucky!

(Her cell phone rings or vibrates.)

Speaking of lucky. My boyfriend. Excuse me.

(Into phone.) Hello, Love.

> *(Pause.)*

What?

> *(Pause.)*

Who?

> *(Her face drops. Pause.)*

Oh, I see.

> *(Pause.)*

Okay.

> *(Pause.)*

I understand. Thank you.

> *(She puts away phone. Turns to tour. Huge smile.)*

That was my boyfriend's cell phone...being used on the other end by...his wife. Excuse me.

> *(She turns her back to tour, pauses, screams.)*

AHHHHHH!

> *(Pause.)*

WHY AM I SO STUPIDDDDD?

> *(She pauses, then turns back around as if nothing happened. Again smiles huge smile.)*

So hey! Who wants to do a couple more? Want to see "New York from the Heights near Brooklyn," a beautiful 1820 watercolor by William Guy Wall, where you can almost see where the Brooklyn Bridge will be... that I may be contemplating throwing myself off of this afternoon? So let's go. Come on. *(Claps hands.)*

Keep up. Everyone keep up! *(Claps hands.)* TOUR'S NOT OVER!

> **(WOMAN** *exits. Lights fade.)*

> *[Production Note: This works very well with an empty white frame upon one easel placed*

stage left and another placed stage right. Remember, imagining these paintings is always funnier than seeing them.]

Joe and Helen Meet
the Roman Art

CHARACTERS

(in order of appearance)

YOUNG ROMAN WOMAN – female, statue

ATLAS – male, statue

POSEIDON – male or female, statue

HERCULES – male, statue

CUSTOMER – small role (can be played by Joe or Helen in disguise)

JOE – male, human

HELEN – female, human

SETTING

Bare stage, three pedestals

TIME

Contemporary

*For a list of artwork in this scene, please see the back of the book.

(Lights rise on museum and four statues: **ATLAS, POSEIDON, HERCULES,** *and* **YOUNG ROMAN WOMAN. ATLAS** *is holding up the world. And there is a small wall right behind them. We hear music playing.** **HERCULES** *starts swaying to the music, followed by* **POSEIDON** *and then* **ATLAS. YOUNG ROMAN WOMAN** *maintains pose.* **ATLAS** *taps* **YOUNG ROMAN WOMAN** *on shoulder, she turns.)*

YOUNG ROMAN WOMAN. Cut it out.

*(***YOUNG ROMAN WOMAN*** goes back to pose.)*

HERCULES. The yearly dinner dance starting up.

ATLAS. Sounds great.

POSEIDON. Won't be long till they start wandering.

HERCULES. Oh yeah.

ATLAS. We'll have a chance to pick one off.

YOUNG ROMAN WOMAN. No.

POSEIDON. Maybe two.

YOUNG ROMAN WOMAN. No, we're not.

MALE STATUES. It's a tradition.

YOUNG ROMAN WOMAN. Well, he better be drunk so no one believes him.

HERCULES. Oh, here comes one.

YOUNG ROMAN WOMAN. Customer!

*(***ALL*** pose. ***CUSTOMER*** enters, obviously drinking, and crosses to ***ATLAS*** statue.)*

---

*A license to produce *You Make Me Frame Shake!* does not include a performance license for any third-party or copyrighted music. Licensees should create an original composition or use music in the public domain. For further information, please see Music Use Note on page 3.

CUSTOMER. Hey, Atlas, how are you? Holding up that thing there. Tickle, tickle, tickle! *(Laughs.)* Tickle, tickle, tickle. *(Laughs.)*

(**HERCULES** *taps* **CUSTOMER** *on shoulder.*)

HERCULES. Excuse me, sir?

(**CUSTOMER** *turns, sees* **HERCULES**, *turns back, screams.*)

CUSTOMER. AHHHHHhhhh!

(**CUSTOMER** *runs out.*)

(*All* **MALE STATUES** *high-five and laugh.*)

YOUNG ROMAN WOMAN. I do not like this at all. And I am officially not participating. Customer!

(*All* **STATUES** *pose.* **JOE** *enters.*)

JOE. Hercules!

(*They break pose.*)

ATLAS. It's just Joe.

YOUNG ROMAN WOMAN. Who?

POSEIDON. Joe Johnson, he works here.

JOE. *(Up to* **HERCULES**.*)* Hercules, I can't do it. Everything we talked about asking Helen to dance, I can't do it.

(*All* **MALE STATUES** *gasp.*)

JOE. *(Looks around.)* I'm sorry, guys. I know you spent a lot of time boosting my confidence.

MALE STATUES. *(Softly.)* You can do it, Joe.

JOE. But I get right up to the moment, she's right in front of me, and I. *(Can't speak.)*

MALE STATUES. *(Sorrowfully.)* OHHH.

JOE. But I have one last plan. I left her a note to meet here at ten. It's five to ten. She should be coming right over.

HERCULES. And what's the plan, Joe?

JOE. Well my last plan is: I'm going to hide behind you and you're going to tell *her* to ask *me* to dance.

HERCULES. That's the plan?

JOE. That's the plan.

HERCULES. That's not a plan, that's called "hiding."

JOE. But I can help when I'm in back of you.

HERCULES.	**POSEIDON.**
No, count us out.	No.

ATLAS. Stupid plan, Joe.

YOUNG ROMAN WOMAN. Customer!

> (**HELEN**, *same age as* **JOE**, *enters and crosses to* **HERCULES**. **HELEN** *is very into her phone, always glancing at it. This fact should allow* **JOE** *his opportunity.*)

JOE. Oh here she comes, please help me.

> (*All* **STATUES** *pose.* **JOE** *crawls behind* **HERCULES**.)

HELEN. (*Crosses to front of* **HERCULES** *statue.*) Oh, hello, Hercules, Atlas, Poseidon.

> (*They break.*)

HERCULES. Hi, Helen.

HELEN. Nice music, isn't it?

HERCULES. Helen, do you find that it's fun to have a dance here at work?

HELEN. Kind of. Except people still keep asking me, "Where's the bathroom."

> (*All* **STATUES** *laugh.*)

But a funny thing just happened...someone left this at my table: "Helen, meet me in front of Hercules, Roman wing, ten p.m."

HERCULES. That's interesting.

HELEN. And typed. How weird.

HERCULES. So, Helen, are you here with anyone?

HELEN. Just my mom. (*About note.*) Who would leave this?

HERCULES. Oh, I thought you were coming with Joe Johnson?

HELEN. No.

ATLAS. I did, too.

POSEIDON. So did I.

HELEN. What gave you that idea?

HERCULES. Oh...you guys are always talking.

POSEIDON. Laughing.

ATLAS. Don't you have lunch sometimes?

HELEN. We do, you're right, we do sometimes. But it seems Joe has a girlfriend.

JOE. No. No, I don't.

HERCULES. No, he doesn't.

HELEN. He's sitting with her.

ATLAS. You're here with a girl?

HELEN. Talking, smiling.

POSEIDON. Joe?

HELEN. Looks like a girlfriend to me.

HERCULES. No, that is not true. It's uh.

HELEN. Oh really? Then who is she, immortal Hercules?

ATLAS. Who is it?

JOE. My cousin.

HERCULES. His cousin.

HELEN. He's dating his cousin?

JOE. I'm not dating my cousin!

HERCULES. NO.

HELEN. Whoa!

JOE. Tell her I'm not.

HELEN. That's creepy.

JOE. She's going to tell everybody I'm dating my cousin.

HELEN. Is that really true, Hercules?

HERCULES. NO! No, he's not dating his cousin; he's just on a date with his cousin.

JOE. I'm not on a date with my cousin.

HELEN. That's like family inbreeding.

HERCULES. No Helen, there is no inbreeding. I know about inbreeding –

JOE. My dad asked her, she's an art major.

HERCULES. Joe's dad invited her; the cousin has nothing to do with Joe.

HELEN. Are you sure?

HERCULES. *(Nods.)* I'm immortal. I'm an inbred. I know these things.

HELEN. Well, Hercules, thanks for the tip.

HERCULES. And if Joe is not going to ask you out, you should ask him out, 'cause I think you have feelings for Joe.

HELEN. Well, between you and I…I do, and he seems like he's going to ask me out, remember I was talking to you about it? But.

JOE. But?

HERCULES. But?

HELEN. He doesn't have any self-confidence.

JOE. True.

HERCULES. True.

HELEN. 'Cause he doesn't realize what a wonderful person he is.

> *(**JOE** perks up.)*

JOE. How so?

HERCULES. How so?

HELEN. Even though he doesn't know much about art.

ALL STATUES. *(Sadly.)* Ohhhhhh!

HERCULES. How do you know that?

JOE. She knows that.

HELEN. But he's such a gentleman; so much fun to be around.

JOE. Really?

HERCULES. Really?

HELEN. Though Joe doesn't know an Etruscan from a Holy Roman Emperor.

ALL STATUES. *(Sadly.)* Ohhhhhhh.

JOE. Etruscans were right after.

ATLAS & POSEIDON. Before!

HELEN. But Joe's sooooo...adorable.

ALL STATUES. *(Happily.)* Hmmmmmm.

JOE. That's the nicest thing anyone's ever said.

HELEN. Okay, I'm going to go back to the party. What a wacky note.

HERCULES. Wait, wait! Before you do.

HELEN. No wonder they didn't show up.

HERCULES. I have one more piece of important advice.

HELEN. *(Her phone rings.)* Oh my phone, who's that?

        *(**HELEN** checks phone.)*

HERCULES. *(To **JOE**.)* You're an idiot.

POSEIDON. She's a wonderful girl.

ATLAS. She thinks you're adorable.

JOE. I know.

HERCULES. Stand up like a man.

POSEIDON. Tell her it's your cousin.

ATLAS. Ask her to dance.

JOE. I'm going to do it.

HERCULES. I'll distract her, you walk around.

JOE. Okay.

HERCULES. Ready?

ATLAS & POSEIDON. Ready?

JOE. I'm ready!

        *(**HELEN** puts phone away.)*

HELEN. My mom just texted me, "Where's the bathroom?"

HERCULES. Helen, one last thing. I need you to close your eyes, count to three, and I have a wonderful surprise for you.

HELEN. Well, okay.

HERCULES. So close your eyes.

HELEN. Okay.

HERCULES. Count to three.

HELEN. One.

ALL STATUES. GO!

>   (**JOE** *stands, circles around the back of* **HELEN**.)

HELEN. Two.

>   (*Pause.*)

   Three.

HERCULES. Open your eyes.

HELEN. And?

HERCULES. And now... And now...

JOE. Oh hi.

HELEN. (*Turns around.*) Oh hi, Joe.

JOE. Hey Helen, thanks for meeting me here.

HELEN. You left this note?

JOE. I did.

HELEN. Why?

JOE. Well, I was wondering.

>   (*Pause.*)

HELEN. Yes?

>   (*The* **STATUES** *mouth and motion the following*
>   *words to* **JOE**.)

ATLAS & POSEIDON. Ask her.

JOE. Uh...I was wondering if.

HERCULES. Come on, Joe.

JOE. Helen?

HELEN. Yeah.

JOE. Would you like to dance?

HELEN. Dance? Really? I thought you're here with your girlfriend?

ALL STATUES. Cous-in!

HELEN. Aren't you here with that girl over there?

ALL STATUES. Say it! NOW!

JOE. Well, she's not my girlfriend, we're related.

HELEN. She's your cousin?

JOE. First cousin. Art major. Dad brought her.

> *(Pause.)*

She'd totally understand.

HELEN. Joe, I have a confession to make too.

JOE. Really?

HELEN. Yeah, couple days ago, you asked me about that Roman head you like to stand near.

JOE. Oh, yeah.

HELEN. I said it was Claudian. I didn't mean that...his name was Claudian.

JOE. Oh.

HELEN. I heard you tell some tourists that.

JOE. You meant the period?

HELEN. There's an emperor: Claudius.

JOE. You are so smart. And I don't know what I'm doing.

HELEN. I should have been clearer.

JOE. I think I told at least three people.

> *(They laugh.)*

I told one guy his name is Claude.

> *(They laugh.)*

> *(Pause.)*

Hey, since we're here, you're here, I'm here, and it's a dance...can I get you to dance...with me?

HELEN. Absolutely.

JOE. Come on.

> *(**JOE** extends his hand, **HELEN** takes it. They exit briskly.)*

YOUNG ROMAN WOMAN. Why were you talking to them? What do those two do here?

ATLAS. They're both guards.

POSEIDON. They were off today.

HERCULES. We'll introduce you tomorrow.

YOUNG ROMAN WOMAN. So they're safe?

ATLAS. They're safe.

HERCULES. Stop worrying about everything, you'll chip your marble.

POSEIDON. Customer.

> *(They pose. A very intoxicated* **CUSTOMER** *enters.)*

CUSTOMER. You know what, marble man; I have wasted half of my wife.

HERCULES. *(Breaks pose.)* Oh yeah, which half?

CUSTOMER. AHHHH! *(Runs out.)*

> *(They all laugh, slap hands.)*

HERCULES. I love doing that.

YOUNG ROMAN WOMAN. No more.

HERCULES. Oh come on.

YOUNG ROMAN WOMAN. That's two tonight!

ATLAS. The dance is once a year.

YOUNG ROMAN WOMAN. Please, I just got out of storage today.

HERCULES. Then live a little.

POSEIDON. Oh look, I can see Joe and Helen dancing.

HERCULES. Oh yeah, right there.

YOUNG ROMAN WOMAN. Oh, look at them.

HERCULES. Hey, he looks like he's going to kiss her.

ATLAS. He is going to kiss her!

POSEIDON. Kiss her!

HERCULES. Kiss her, Joe.

MALE STATUES. Kiss her! Kiss her! Kiss her!

> *(***MALE STATUES** *deflate: No kiss...)*

Ohhh.

POSEIDON. He's not going to kiss her.

HERCULES. That'll take another year.

YOUNG ROMAN WOMAN. I can't believe this.

ATLAS. They make a nice couple though.

HERCULES. I love the yearly dinner dance.

POSEIDON. Me, too.

ATLAS. It's a nice time.

HERCULES. And tonight we weren't just scaring people.

ATLAS. No! We actually helped two of them.

POSEIDON. Huh, imagine that.

ATLAS. We're like a force for good.

HERCULES. Hey! Everybody put your hands in.

> (**HERCULES**, **ATLAS**, *and* **POSEIDON** *put hands in.* **YOUNG ROMAN WOMAN** *does not.*)

MALE STATUES. One, two, three! BREAK! YEAH!

HERCULES. FIRST CENTURY STATUUUUUES!

MALE STATUES. We're number ONE! We're number ONE!

YOUNG ROMAN WOMAN. Customer!

> (*They all freeze. Lights fade. Blackout.*)

End of Play

Optional:
Babes in the Bernini

CHARACTERS

MARIO – male
GINA – female

SETTING

Bare stage

TIME

Present

AUTHOR'S NOTE

If you need to cut down the play, cut a larger scene and put in this shorter, optional scene. Or just put this scene in the play, too. I'll leave that up to you and would love to hear your ideas on this.

*For a list of artwork in this scene, please see the back of the book.

*(Lights rise on **MARIO**.)*

MARIO. First day working at the museum, standing in front
of the painting of the goddess Echo,
I noticed a beautiful woman on my right. So I turn.
Smile. She says:

*(Lights come up on **GINA** in background.)*

GINA. Beautiful, isn't it?

MARIO. To which I say, "What, what."

*(**GINA** giggles.)*

MARIO. We talk a little. Walk a little. Had lunch.

(Pause.)

And that's how I met Gina, the girl of my dreams.

(Pause.)

And then I lost her number.

(Pause.)

I don't know where it went. I asked everyone. Personnel
told me that she left the museum. They couldn't give
me any other info. I was crushed. And it wasn't until
I met an overly serene woman, who spells her name:
K. A. L. M. who works in and is a perfect match for
a Cambodian, mid-eleventh century, bronze statue
named: "Kneeling Female," that my confidence came
back. Kalm said she couldn't go out on Saturday 'cause
of dance class. Then one Saturday, one of my friends
had a birthday party at a Greco-Turkish restaurant, out
come the belly dancers. And there she is. There's Kalm.
And she wasn't that calm. She was actually pretty
revealing in her finger cymbals. I excused myself, took
a cab home. Never told her. I just said that I'm taking
classes of my own. And then I met Aria in Musical

Instruments. A babe in charge of Shaman raven rattles to Benny Goodman's clarinet. We went out for a month. Till I met a friend of hers when we were walking around at a Beatle fest. The friend turned out to be her husband. She tried to explain they live separately. Which sent me reeling into Cassandra. An associate in costumes who is obsessed with masquerade parties. She has the Raimundo de Madrazo y Garreta painting "Masqueraders" tattooed on her back. Cassandra and her masquerading friends would jump in fountains, dance on tables. They were crazy. And when I asked Cassandra if we could go out on a date without masks and her friends...she dumped me. And two of her friends, Harlequin and Zanni, I swear those were their names, sent me a decree stating that I was exiled from "The Lapin Agile Association."

After that, I swore never to date anyone who worked within a one-mile radius of Eighty-fourth and Fifth. Until I was standing in front of the statue: "Bacchanal: A Faun Teased by Children" by Bernini. I felt a tap on my shoulder. A voice asked:

(Lights rise on **GINA** *in background.)*

GINA. Do you work here?

MARIO. And there stood Gina, who I met my first day at work in front of the goddess Echo. I apologized profusely. I explained how I begged personnel for any info. She explained she is working at the Frick Museum down the street. I was shocked. And that she saw me a few weeks later.

GINA. Hey, I was going to say hello but you were on a date with that belly dancer Kalm.

MARIO. How did you know she was a belly dancer?

GINA. Then a month later, I was cutting though Central Park and saw you seemed to be busy hitting on some of the married women who work here.

MARIO. I did not know Aria was married.

GINA. Anyway, I thought I'd say hi since I heard from a friend, one of the associates in Costumes...do you know Cassandra?

MARIO. Yes.

GINA. That she dumped you.

MARIO. I paused. I looked at the Bernini statue. It is a fawn in the shape of a man being teased by three children. And the faun is being treated so divinely, so spiritually exalted by the tease that he's giving in. I turned back to Gina and said, "In fact, I was rejected by the entire Lapin Agile Masquerader's Association."

GINA. You're too cute for a mask.

MARIO. We talk a little. Walk a little. Memorized her number. We've been dating two years now. I'm finishing up my master's at Columbia, Gina's finishing hers at NYU. Sometimes when we walk around we'll find ourselves back in front of the goddess Echo. That's where I belong.

(*Pause.*)

I guess we all have our Bernini moments.

(*Pause.*)

I'm just really glad that's over.

(*Lights fade. Blackout.*)

LIST OF ARTWORK BY SCENE

See www.LuigiJannuzzi.com for pictures/links.

ACT ONE

1. Part I: Another Misguided Tour

"The Heart of the Andes," 1859, Frederic Edwin Church

"The Rocky Mountains, Lander's Peak," 1863, Albert Bierstadt

2. Lusting After Monet

"Camille Monet on a Garden Bench," 1873, Claude Monet

"Jean Monet on his Hobby Horse," 1872, Claude Monet

3. The Tray Picker-Upper in the Met Café

"A Waitress at Duval's Restaurant," 1875, Auguste Renoir

4. Part II: Another Misguided Tour

"Siyotanka" (Sioux courting flute from Catlinite), 1900, named for George Catlin

5. Dating Roman Art

"The Marble statue of a youthful Hercules," Early Imperial Flavian Period, 69-96 A.D., Roman

"Atlas Supporting the Globe," 1780, French

"Bronze statuette of Neptune," Early Imperial Period, 1st century A.D., Roman

"Marble statue of a girl," Imperial Period, 1st or 2nd century A.D., Roman

"Marble statue of a wounded Amazon," Imperial Period, 1st or 2nd century A.D., Roman

"Marble sarcophagus with the Triumph of Dionysos and the Seasons," Late Imperial Gallienic Period, 260-270 A.D., Roman

"Marble Statue Group of the Three Graces," Imperial Period, 1st or 2nd century A.D., Roman

"Bronze chariot inlaid with ivory," Archaic Period, 6th century B.C., Etruscan

"Bronze statuette of a veiled and masked dancer," Hellenistic Period, 3rd or 2nd century B.C., Greek

6. Two Children Teasing a Cat

"Two Children Teasing a Cat," 1587-88, Annibale Carracci

"The Abduction of the Sabine Women," 1633-34, Nicolas Poussin

"A Hypocrite and a Slanderer," 1770-83, Franz Messerschmidt

"The Rabbit Hunters," 1850, Thomas Hewes Hinckley

"The Unicorn is Attacked (from the Unicorn Tapestries),"
1495-1505, South Netherlandish

"Unicorns (Legend-Sea Calm)," 1906, Arthur B. Davies

"Salome with the Head of Saint John the Baptist,"
1507-09, Andrea Solario

Search "Cannibal art at the Metropolitan Museum of Art"

7. Stuck in the Middle With You

"Antoine-Laurent Lavoisier and His Wife," 1788, Jacques-Louis David

"Ruins of the Tuileries Palace," 19th century, Isidore Pils

"The Garden of the Tuileries on a Spring Morning,"
1899, Camille Pissarro

"Severed head, said to be that of Maximilien-François-Marie-Isidore
de Robespierre," 1794, Vivant Denon

"Madame Élisabeth de France," 1787, Adélaïde Labille-Guiard

"The Death of Socrates," 1787, Jacques-Louis David

8. Part III: Another Misguided Tour

Any John James Audubon print at the Met

9. Another Fertility God Fugue

"Seated Couple," 18th-early 19th century, Mali,
southern cliff, Dogon peoples

"Mother and Child," 15th-20th century, Mali,
Bougouni or Dioila region, Bamana peoples

ACT TWO

1. Broken Eggs

"Broken Eggs," 1756, Jean-Baptiste Greuze

2. Part IV: Another Misguided Tour

"View from Mount Holyoke, Northampton, Massachusetts, after a Thunderstorm – The Oxbow," 1836, Thomas Cole

3. Here Sphinxie, Sphinxie!

"Aristotle with a Bust of Homer," 1653, Rembrandt

"Oedipus and the Sphinx," 1864, Gustave Moreau

"Marble stele (grave marker) of a youth and a little girl," Archaic Period, 530 B.C., Greek

"Young Woman Peeling Apples," 1655, Nicolaes Maes

"The Thinker," 1910, Auguste Rodin

"Adam," 1910, Auguste Rodin

"Perseus with the Head of Medusa," 1804-06, Antonio Canova

"Ugolino and His Sons," 1865-67, Jean-Baptiste Carpeaux

"Diana," 1894, Augustus Saint-Gaudens

4. Part V: Another Misguided Tour

"Still Life: Fruit," 1855, Severin Roesen

"Still Life with Fruit," 1857, John F. Francis

"Still Life with Lobster and Fruit," early 1650s, Abraham van Beyeren

"The Silver Tureen," 1728-30, Jean-Baptiste-Siméon Chardin

5. The Art of Detention

"Soap Bubbles," 1733-34, Jean-Baptiste-Siméon Chardin

"Diana," 1892-93, Augustus Saint-Gaudens

"The Lacemaker," 1656, Nicolaes Maes

6. Thought – A Love Story

"The Thinker," 1910, Auguste Rodin

7. Part VI: Another Misguided Tour

"Fur Traders Descending the Missouri," 1845, George Caleb Bingham

"New York from the Heights near Brooklyn," 1820-23, William Guy Wall

8. Joe and Helen Meet the Roman Art

"Marble statue of a girl," Imperial Period, 1st or 2nd century A.D., Roman

"Marble statue of a youthful Hercules," Early Imperial Flavian Period, 69-96 A.D., Roman

"Hercules or Atlas Supporting the Globe," 1780, French

"Bronze statuette of neptune," Early Imperial Period,
1st century A.D., Roman

"Marble head of a youth," Early Imperial Claudian Period,
41-54 A.D., Roman

Optional Scene: Babes in the Bernini

"Echo," 1874, Alexandre Cabanel

"Kneeling Female," Angkor Period, 11th century, Cambodian

"Shaman Raven Rattle," 19th century, Native American

"Masqueraders," 1875-78, Raimundo de Madrazo y Garreta

"At the Lapin Agile," 1905, Pablo Picasso

"Bacchanal: A Faun Teased by Children," 1616-17, Gian Lorenzo Bernini